Praise for *Pray First*

"There's no one better to lead you into a deeper relationship with God through prayer than my friend Chris Hodges. *Pray First* isn't just another book release, it's a lifestyle Pastor Chris models consistently and the engine behind the phenomenal breadth and impact of his ministry. Get ready to have your entire life revolutionized as you begin to pray first!"

—LOUIE GIGLIO, PASTOR, PASSION CITY CHURCH/PASSION CONFERENCES; AUTHOR, *DON'T GIVE THE ENEMY A SEAT AT YOUR TABLE*

"From cover to cover Pastor Chris Hodges is just so practical and points you directly to what God's Word says about prayer. What an incredible resource and necessary reminder that prayer isn't about being more 'religious,' but it is all about a relationship that our heavenly Father craves to have with us."

—SADIE ROBERTSON HUFF, AUTHOR, SPEAKER, AND FOUNDER OF LIVE ORIGINAL

"Many people believe in the power of prayer but lack the confidence to pray boldly. In his new book, *Pray First,* Pastor Chris Hodges takes an in-depth look at the kinds of prayers that touch the heart of God. This book will spiritually motivate and equip readers to get to know God more intimately through a rich and meaningful life of prayer."

—CRAIG GROESCHEL, PASTOR, LIFE.CHURCH; AUTHOR, *DANGEROUS PRAYERS*

"I've heard it said, 'When we work, we work, but when we pray, God works.' In this insightful and extraordinary book, Pastor Chris practically guides us in taking steps to put prayer in its proper place: a first response and not a last resort."

—DR. DHARIUS DANIELS, AUTHOR, *RELATIONAL INTELLIGENCE*; LEAD PASTOR, CHANGE CHURCH

"Prayer changes everything. Prayer is heaven's Wi-Fi and Chris Hodges is the brilliant technician connecting us with God's life-changing 5G network. In *Pray First* you'll receive a powerful activation manual that will ignite a prayer life that will prompt heaven to invade your earth."

—SAMUEL RODRIGUEZ, NEW SEASON LEAD PASTOR

"I have been greatly inspired by the life of Chris Hodges, especially his prayer life and his emphasis of prayer at Church of the Highlands. In *Pray First*, Pastor Chris seeks to dismantle the obstacles to prayer that we create in our hearts and minds. This book aims to empower readers and set in motion a life where prayer is a lifestyle and meaningful conversations with God are daily. I would wholeheartedly recommend this book to anyone looking to grow in their relationship with God and being more active in prayer with all areas of their life."

—CHAD VEACH, PASTOR, ZOE CHURCH LA; AUTHOR, *WORRIED ABOUT EVERYTHING BECAUSE I PRAY ABOUT NOTHING*

"Is there anything more important in our relationship with God than a life of prayer? I don't think so. . . . I am so grateful for Chris Hodges and the book *Pray First*! It has inspired me and given me a renewed heart and vision for my relationship with prayer and, ultimately, with God. Through the highs and lows of this life, we were created to walk and talk with our Creator. This book is the North Star pointing us and guiding us to a fulfilled life of prayer."

—CHRIS TOMLIN, ARTIST, SONGWRITER, AUTHOR

"When I think of the words 'Pray First' I think of Pastor Chris Hodges. He has lived this message for thirty-nine years and it has deeply impacted our church in Miami and countless communities around the globe. The prayer models shared within will bring practical guidance to your conversations with God and his wisdom on corporate and personal prayer will awaken your heart to yearn for all that awaits in God's presence. Forever grateful for this life message!"

—RICH WILKERSON JR., VOUS CHURCH

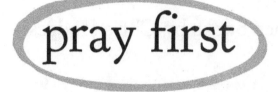

pray first

the transformative power
of a life built on prayer

Other Books by Chris Hodges

The Daniel Dilemma

The Daniel Dilemma Study Guide

What's Next?

What's Next? Study Guide

Out of the Cave

Out of the Cave Study Guide

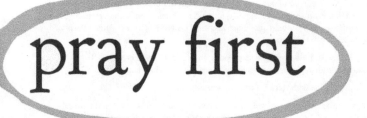

pray first

the transformative power
of a life built on prayer

CHRIS HODGES

NELSON
BOOKS

An Imprint of Thomas Nelson

ISBN 978-1-4002-2130-1 (eBook)
ISBN 978-1-4002-2129-5 (TP)

Library of Congress Control Number: 2022946403

Printed and bound in the UK using 100% Renewable Electricity at CPI Group (UK) Ltd

23 24 25 26 27   CPI   10 9 8 7 6 5 4 3 2

This book is dedicated to my personal intercessors:
Hamp Greene, Colette Greene, Jim Laffoon, Gary Larson,
Sherrill Larson, Kirby Sevier, and Tim Spurlock.
Your prayers have covered me.
Your love and support has comforted me.
You have fought with me and for me in the heavenly realms.
Your prayers have made all the difference.
You have my loving gratitude.

Contents

PART 3: PRAYER AND FASTING

Introduction

Make Prayer Your First Response— Not Your Last Resort

Prayer is easier than you think and
more important than you realize.

Prayer is often the most misunderstood part of following
Jesus.

Many people view prayer as if it's an innate talent. You may
not even realize you hold this perception, but your thoughts and
actions reveal otherwise. You've learned to pray because you grew
up in church or because that's what your family did, but it still
seems awkward and unfamiliar. Prayer seems like athletic speed,
musical talent, or a quick sense of humor: some are born with it
and others are not. So you admire people who pray with confident
ease and do what you can to get by because you've always heard
that prayer is such an important part of being a Christian. But you

feel like you're not much good at it and consign praying to church services and mealtimes.

Or maybe you regard prayer as more of an acquired skill. Being a prayer warrior is simply a matter of putting in the time and effort, you think, so you practice daily and constantly try new techniques to improve your prayer life. You view it as a spiritual discipline—which it is of course—but it has never become something you particularly enjoy or do spontaneously.

Others consider prayer as a supernatural SOS, a cry for help when they don't know what to do or find themselves desperately in need of help. When you lose your job or the car breaks down, when the medical tests come back positive or your child's addiction reveals itself—*that's* when you pray because circumstances are suddenly overwhelming.

Based on what I've experienced and witnessed in nearly forty years in ministry, I believe people *know* they should pray and *want* to pray, but don't really understand what to do. We have plenty of books on prayer, perhaps more than any other topic in the faith-based category. Inspiration isn't the problem—most of us are sufficiently inspired and want to make prayer central to our relationship with God.

Many people don't have a working definition of prayer. Prayer is simply talking with and listening to God. That's it!

Yet, even if we have that working definition of prayer, we still don't know what to say when we pray. We don't know how to prioritize prayer in our lives.

I often overhear people, especially in hospital waiting rooms, say, "Well, I guess there's nothing left to do but pray." Similarly,

I've met with families in crisis and heard the same refrain. While sometimes prayer is the *only* thing we can do, it is always the *best* thing we can do.

Too often, prayer becomes our last resort.

But God wants prayer to be our first response.

Lifeblood of Faith

The importance of prayer in sustaining and strengthening our faith cannot be overestimated. If we define prayer as connecting with God and confronting the Enemy, then prayer ought to be an ongoing conversation with God about every area of our lives. In the Bible prayer is not mentioned occasionally as an option or consideration; prayer is essential to knowing God. We're told to "pray continually" (1 Thessalonians 5:17 NIV) and to be "faithful in prayer" (Romans 12:12 NIV), not just sporadically or on Sundays or when we feel like it.

Praying continually may sound challenging or even impossible, but connecting with God in the midst of every part of your day is more than worth it:

- **Prayer overcomes anxiety and fear.** Prayer keeps us anchored in truth and helps us maintain an eternal perspective, freeing us from circumstantial worries and temporary trials. "Do not be anxious about anything," we're instructed, "but in every situation, by prayer and petition, with thanksgiving, present your requests to

God" (Philippians 4:6 NIV). When you immerse yourself in regular prayer, "the peace of God, which transcends all understanding, will guard your hearts and your minds in Christ Jesus" (Philippians 4:7 NIV). Prayer is a place to "offload" cares and give them to God.

- **Prayer connects us with God.** Prayer keeps your faith alive, your hope in Christ strong, and your relationship with God healthy. If prayer is the lifeblood of the Christian faith, then I'm afraid many believers are anemic. We know prayer is essential to our faith but still struggle to make it part of our daily lives. Prayer intimidates us. Despite all we've heard and learned, we still feel uncomfortable praying, whether in private or in public. Prayer feels old-fashioned and quaint to some, while others consider prayer sacred and unfathomable.

> **If prayer is the lifeblood of the Christian faith, then I'm afraid many believers are anemic.**

God wants us to view prayer as the vibrant foundation of our relationship with Him. A lifestyle of prayer is the secret to an authentic Christian life. How do we make prayer a lifestyle? By weaving it into the fabric of our daily lives as we make it the priority God intended. Once we realize how talking and listening to God draws us closer, we enjoy the intimacy we've longed to experience. Only then can we know the peace that passes all human understanding (Philippians 4:7) and take shelter in the unconditional love of our heavenly Father (Romans 8:38–39).

- **Prayer reveals God's purpose for our lives.** Prayer can change us from the inside out as we experience more of who God is and less of who we are. Curiously enough, though, prayer also helps us become more our true selves, more authentic as we discover God's unique purpose for our time here on earth.

- **Prayer empowers us to live supernaturally.** Relying on our relationship with God is the only way to accomplish all that He has created us to do in this life. Prayer is necessary because God calls us to do things that we can never accomplish on our own. In order to rely on His power continually, we need to be in constant communication. We need His help because our efforts aren't adequate. All of us have areas of our lives where we need God's help to pull it off, to persevere, to push through and do what we know He wants done. The good news is that God never intended us to live naturally. He wants us to live *supernaturally*. Prayer is that access point, where heaven touches earth, where we maintain our lifeline with our Creator, our Savior, and our Redeemer.

You don't have to take my word for it—consider God's. His Word urges us, "Rejoice always, pray continually, give thanks in all circumstances; for this is God's will for you in Christ Jesus" (1 Thessalonians 5:16–18 NIV). In the early church, followers of Jesus "all joined together constantly in prayer, along with the women and Mary the mother of Jesus, and with his brothers" (Acts 1:14 NIV). New believers "devoted themselves to the apostles'

Prayer is that access point, where heaven touches earth, where we maintain our lifeline with our Creator, our Savior, and our Redeemer.

teaching and to fellowship, to the breaking of bread and to prayer" (Acts 2:42 NIV).

Most compelling of all is the example and instruction Jesus gave us on prayer. Throughout His life and ministry, Christ retreated to quiet places for private time with His Father. Taking note of their Master's example, the disciples asked Jesus to teach them to pray, and the outline for prayer He gave them in response is what we call the Lord's Prayer (Matthew 6:9–13). This model demonstrates how prayer can address all areas of our lives as we connect to God and immerse ourselves in His perspective.

Tethered Together

What would it look like if you brought God into every area of your life throughout each day? The key in allowing prayer to permeate your life is to put it first, literally. When the Bible instructs us to pray continually or constantly, the emphasis is not on perpetual repetition but on importance and consistency. God wants us to *pray first* in any and all situations. He wants us to thank Him, ask Him, trust Him, seek Him, listen to Him, and enjoy all the blessings He gives.

- When you wake up in the morning, pray first and thank God for the day ahead.
- Before you go to sleep at night, pray first and praise Him for getting you through the day's demands.
- When you're leaving your home for school, pray first.

- Merging onto the busy highway, pray first.
- About to lead the Zoom meeting at work, pray first.
- Reconnecting with a friend over coffee, pray first.
- Helping your kids with homework, pray first.
- Waiting in the doctor's office, pray first.
- Paying for groceries at the store, pray first.

No matter what you're doing throughout your day, praying first keeps you tethered to the One who loves you most.

Prayer is not just for Sunday school and mealtimes. It is not to be reserved only for your daily quiet times. Prayer is for *all times*. Communicating with God throughout your day brings Him into everything and everyone you encounter—your spouse and kids, your boss and coworkers, friends and neighbors, baristas and customer service reps, delivery people and mechanics, bankers and teachers.

When you pray first, you keep in constant contact with Almighty God, the Creator of heaven and earth, who also happens to be your Abba Father, your lavishly loving Papa. When you pray first, you have access to God the Father through Jesus the Son, who has paid the price for your sin and now intercedes on your behalf without ceasing. When you pray first, the Holy Spirit sticks with you closer than any friend. He'll help you pray even when you don't know how to express yourself with words.

When you pray first, your faith matures and you bear the spiritual fruit God has planted in you.

Prayer Matters

I wrote this book to help you experience the full abundance of the Christian life. While I would never presume to call myself an expert, I humbly offer all I've learned in many decades of personal practice and public teaching. The first section of this book will help you make prayer an unshakeable priority in practical ways—by focusing on a place, a plan, and the Persons (Father, Son, and Holy Spirit) with whom you're communicating.

Next, we'll look at different models of prayer drawn from Scripture, including the Lord's Prayer, the Prayer of Moses, the Prayer of Jabez, and others for protection, provision, and power in overcoming the Enemy. By studying the situation, intention, and outcome of these various prayers, we will see how they apply to us and our conversations with God.

Our third and final section focuses on the often-misunderstood pairing of fasting with praying. We will explore the link between these two spiritually related exercises and discover how they facilitate intimacy with Him in unique ways. You may be surprised to discover how fasting can help take prayer to a deeper place of spiritual intimacy between you and God.

For years our church has practiced 21 Days of Prayer twice each year. In January we pray with an emphasis on fasting, and in August we pray with an emphasis on reaching people with the life-giving message of Jesus. When people ask me the secret to our enormous growth and expanding impact, I never fail to mention the vital importance of being people who pray—and take prayer seriously enough to fast. Based on our experiences, I'll share an easy-to-follow 21-day plan to help you incorporate fasting as part of your practice of prayer. We'll look at different kinds of fasts and how to practice each in a healthy manner.

Having the right prayer resources at the right times has made a huge difference in my relationship with God and how I live my life. I've written *Pray First* in hopes it will be this kind of relevant, how-to resource for you. I want you to see how prayer naturally envelops all aspects of your life when you make it a consistent, deliberate part of your daily routines.

Regardless of what you think about prayer, how often or how little you pray, or what your past experience has been, it's time to discover the depth of joy, peace, and purpose that only comes when you *pray first*!

part one

Learning About Prayer

Prayer is the difference between the best
you can do and the best God can do.

one

the priority of prayer

———————

It's not "all's well that ends well"—
it's "all's well that begins well"!

People often flash their bracelets at me.

Just the other day I was coming out of Lowe's when I heard someone shout across the parking lot, "Hey, Pastor Chris!" Beaming with pride, a man in jeans and a T-shirt held up his arm and with his other hand pointed to a familiar rubber bracelet on his wrist.

"Hey," I yelled back, returning his smile. "Pray first!"

"Pray first!" he echoed before turning to load the rest of his purchases into his truck.

As strange as it may sound, there's no greeting I enjoy

hearing more than "pray first." You are likely aware of the popular practice of wearing colorful bracelets with a name or slogan on them to show support for a particular cause or to remind others of someone or something significant. Several years ago I was preaching on the importance of putting prayer first in our lives, and someone on our team suggested making hundreds of rubber-band bracelets inscribed with PRAY FIRST on them.

We had no idea if these bracelets would catch on, but we ran out that first Sunday they were available and have ordered thousands more in the years since. I urge people to wear it, remember it, and do it—no matter who they are or what they are doing. As a result, "pray first" has become an enduring anthem at our church, a kind of rallying cry, and I always love it when I catch a glimpse of one of our bracelets on someone at the store, in a restaurant, or at a ball game.

Granted, it's not the bracelet that's significant—it's the message to make prayer your first priority.

Child's Play

Your prayer life anchors your relationship with God. Yet so many believers seem to struggle with the daily practice of prayer. They consider prayer to be something they know God wants them to do, but it feels awkward and a little scary. After all, how do you talk with the God of the universe? So they come to God in prayer like a nervous defendant approaching the stern judge in a courtroom or like Dorothy apprehensively stepping before the Mighty Oz in his smoke-filled inner sanctum.

But God doesn't want prayer to be this formal kind of communication that requires particular words and proper phrases. We may feel afraid to reach out to God, thinking He will judge us or that He won't reveal Himself to us. But He's not judging us; His Son has already lived the perfect life and made the sacrifice to pay for our sins. He's not hiding behind smoke and mirrors or remaining aloof and distant. God simply wants us to talk with Him, to tell Him everything, to ask for His help, to thank Him for all our blessings, to trust Him with our pain—and all our other emotions too. God is ready to welcome us to an ongoing conversation with Him. He doesn't want us to be a nervous wreck trying to perform or deliver a monologue. He simply wants our whole hearts to depend on Him and rest in Him.

Think about the children in your life and how they communicate with you. Depending on their age and stage, the words they use may vary, but their open, loving, unselfconscious style is often the same. It's one of the things I love most about being a grandfather, or Papa, as our grandkids call me. "Papa, do you want to play?" or "Papa, look what I drew!" or "Here I come, Papa!" sounds like music to my ears. Their faces light up with bright eyes and wide smiles as if they couldn't be happier to see me and talk with me.

I wonder if little ones' communication style is one of the reasons why Jesus told us that we must be like children in order to know God.

He called a little child to him, and placed the child among them. And he said: "Truly I tell you, unless you change and become like little children, you will never enter the kingdom of heaven. Therefore, whoever takes the lowly position of this child is the greatest in the kingdom of heaven." (Matthew 18:2–4 NIV)

Based on this truth, we could learn a few things from children about how to approach God in prayer. After all, through our relationship with Jesus, we have received the Holy Spirit and become adopted heirs. We are God's own children who are urged to cry out, "Abba, Father"—a heart cry to a loving Father (Romans 8:15). Rather than viewing God as distant and unrelatable, we can approach Him as a parent who lavishly loves His children.

Children are innocent and humble, unassuming and eager to share their experience of the world and to bask in their parents' loving attention. Kids want to be seen and heard, to be valued and protected and appreciated. They know communication is essential to make their needs known. However, as adults I suspect most of us don't relate to God in this way. Instead we make communication with Him more difficult than it needs to be.

But what if prayer is easier than you think?

Start Fresh

In addition to how we think about our approach to God in prayer, we may consider prayer a kind of one-and-done activity, something we do on Sundays at church or before mealtimes. Maybe we say the Lord's Prayer at certain events or pray for someone battling illness. Prayer has a place in our lives, maybe even a regular place, but it's limited by our narrow view of the Christian life.

For people who grew up in the church, dislodging this compartmentalized view of prayer can be challenging. In the South where I grew up, most people went to church, said they were Christians, and prayed when they were supposed to pray. Praying was like singing hymns, observing Communion, or collecting the tithes and offerings—part of "church stuff" that had its place but wasn't all that relevant in daily life.

Other people tell me they grew up in a religion or faith system that focused on set prayers as part of a liturgy, a regular order of service based on the seasonal church calendar. They memorized the necessary prayers, recited them together at the appropriate times in the service, and didn't think about them again until the next service. Based on their experience, they viewed the prayers they learned as something similar to the Pledge of Allegiance or a well-known poem—culturally, historically, and religiously significant but not personally relevant.

Yet others tell me that learning to pray is like learning a new language. They have none of the baggage from their upbringing that others may have, but they feel like a tourist trying to learn native phrases while on an exotic vacation. Praying makes them feel uncomfortable and self-conscious, especially in public or with other people. They want to know the basics of how to pray without embarrassment but struggle to find clear biblical models or helpful answers to their questions.

Regardless of your past associations and prayer practices, it's time to approach it with a fresh desire to draw closer to God.

What's the Frequency?

While we may be tempted to say God prefers quality over quantity when it comes to our prayers, I believe He wants both. The Bible makes it clear that emphasizing quantity alone is not the point. This kind of score-keeping becomes legalistic, detached, and obligatory. Praying just to check it off your to-do list misses the point and loses an opportunity to connect to your supernatural power source.

Some people slip into praying this way without even realizing it. When they first committed to following Christ, maybe they learned to have a quiet time first thing every morning. Perhaps they were told it should include reading a devotional, a psalm, a passage from the Gospels, or some other certain sequence. They might have been instructed to thank God for three things before they asked Him for one.

Having a model and sequence to your prayers is not a bad thing, as we'll explore in part 2. But when you cling to the way you were instructed to pray as a safety net to make sure you're a good Christian, then the emphasis has shifted. Instead of drawing closer to the Lord, praising and worshiping Him, and getting to know Him more intimately, you have focused on doing a job, completing a task, and moving on to apparently more important matters. This would be like having a date night with your spouse but not enjoying each other's company. Instead, you are merely going through the motions because it's supposed to be good for your marriage.

If keeping count is not the answer, then you might think it doesn't matter how often you pray, as long as you engage whole-heartedly when you do. This conclusion could be drawn from noticing how certain people in the Bible pray for specific purposes. Noah prayed in thanksgiving and praise when the floodwaters receded and he and his family once again stepped on dry land (Genesis 8:18–20). Hannah prayed diligently for the Lord to give her a child, which He did—her son and God's prophet Samuel (1 Samuel 1:9–19). Elijah prayed boldly for God to demonstrate His power over the false idols of Israel's king and queen (1 Kings 18:36–37).

However, we see Jesus demonstrating both quality and con-sistency in His prayer life. Throughout his public ministry, Jesus knew the importance of getting away from the clamor of the crowds to connect with His Father: "Very early in the morning, while it was still dark, Jesus got up, left the house and went off to a solitary place, where he prayed" (Mark 1:35 NIV). Over and over, we see this pattern of Jesus making time to pray alone (Matthew 14:23; Luke 9:18, 22:39–41).

Keep in mind, though, that these are not the only times Jesus prayed—nor likely the other individuals mentioned. Prayer was so closely interwoven into their lives that it blanketed all areas of who they were and what they did. We find at least three dozen mentions in the Gospels of Jesus praying. He prayed in public (John 11:41–42), before choosing His disciples (Luke 6:12–13), before healing people (Mark 7:34–35), after healing people (Luke 5:13–16), and when feeding the 5,000 (John 6:11). Jesus also taught on prayer and gave us the perfect outline for how to pray, which we'll later explore in great detail (Matthew 18).

Prayer must be a priority if you hope to cultivate a lifestyle of prayer.

Engaging purposefully *and* daily is key.

Without Ceasing

In the early church, followers of Jesus devoted themselves to prayer (Acts 2:42) and prayed continuously: "They all joined together constantly in prayer, along with the women and Mary the mother of Jesus, and with his brothers" (Acts 1:14 NIV). The apostle Paul urged, "Rejoice always, pray without ceasing, give thanks in all circumstances; for this is the will of God in Christ Jesus for you" (1 Thessalonians 5:16–18 ESV).

"Pray as much as you can while you're doing everything else!"

If this amount of praying sounds unreasonable, if not impossible, to you, don't worry—you're not alone. A new believer once asked me, "How can I pray all the time and still get everything else done?" My answer to him reflects how I interpret the emphasis in these passages—making prayer a priority: "Pray as much as you can while you're doing everything else!"

If prayer is meant to be communion with God, then if we do everything we do with God in mind—remaining mindful of His presence with us, His purpose for us, and His image in everyone we meet—then we can pray without ceasing, without it even being a question of quantity. This is how we pray "without ceasing." Otherwise, it may just turn into a game of tallying how many times we talk to God with our words rather than living in prayerful communion with God, which could ultimately become an improper reliance on works rather than receiving the gracious gift of His presence with us all the time. There's no "right amount" of times to pray—that's the point of learning to pray first. To make it practical, I pray one-sentence prayers throughout the day— literally in every situation. It's a constant conversation with God.

The goal is to make prayer a priority so that you don't miss out on deepening your relationship with God and enjoying all the benefits that go with it. Making it a priority requires being intentional and deliberate, which involves having a place and making a plan—and we'll discuss both in upcoming chapters. Keep in mind, however, that the goal of being focused and committed to prayer is *relationship*, not *religion*. Prayer is about our personal relationship with a personal God—who is the Father, Son, and Holy Spirit—not fulfilling a mandatory ritual for its own sake.

Making prayer a priority ensures that you won't minimize it as simply your default SOS. While prayer is not *less* than turning to God for help in a time of need, we have to remember that prayer is so much *more*. So often we act first, and only when we experience the consequences or face the unexpected do we ask God to bail us out. Prayer is not about living life on your own terms until you realize your limitations and then turning to God.

Prayer is about living in connection to God and, through that

The goal of being focused and committed to prayer is *relationship*, not *religion*.

connection, living out His purpose for your life, which is why it's important to talk to God before you act, before you decide, before you're tempted, before you speak, before you risk.

Think for a moment: How would your life be different if you were to *pray first before everything you do*?

First Things First

Although we are to pray throughout the day, I believe starting each day with prayer is paramount to keeping it your priority. I've been faithful to give God the first part of each day for more than forty years. Trust me, that says much more about Him than me. Praying each morning before my day gets started helps me connect to my Father first thing. I want Him to know that He is the most important thing in my day and in my life. It's not just that I'm praying—I'm praying first!

God wants to be first. He wants to be the center of our attention, our affection, our attitude, and our actions. God told the people of Israel, "You shall have no other gods before me" (Exodus 20:3 NIV), and the same command applies to us. When we give God the first of anything—our income, our time, our attention, our energy—we declare that God is first in our lives. What we have—*everything* we have—belongs to Him and it comes from Him. We honor God by our first practices.

There are many ways you can communicate the honor of priority in your relationship with the Lord. Going to church on the first day of the week shows that He takes priority over your entire week. Paying your tithe before you pay bills or make purchases is another way. And praying first thing in the morning—regardless of whether you're a morning person or not, regardless of whether it fits your schedule or not—shows God that nothing comes before Him. Because praying first is not just for you and your benefit.

Praying first honors God.

Keep Talking

In every situation you face on any given day, consider the difference if you prayed first. Before getting out of bed in the morning, pray in thanksgiving for a good night's rest and ask in advance for blessings and guidance for the day ahead. Before the kids leave for school, pray for them to remain safe, for them to gain knowledge and wisdom, and for them to reflect God's love. First thing when you get in the car, thank God when it starts, and ask for protection on the highway.

Just imagine the rest of your day and all the demands, roles, and responsibilities of your life right now. Quiet times of intimate talks with God are wonderful and necessary, but prayers-on-the-run may be more practical on a daily basis. Pray first and then click to join the big Zoom meeting at work. Pray first and then take the dog to the vet. Pray first and then check your balance online. Pray first and then finish your studies. Pray first and then cook dinner.

When the unexpected happens, before you start panicking and wondering how you will pay the bill, heal the wound, fix the fridge, find your next job, or repair the relationship—you guessed it—pray first. Maybe you are already in a difficult situation and feel like you don't know what to say to God. You haven't prayed because you're afraid of what you really want to say to Him. That's okay—He can handle anything you give Him.

God wants you to come to Him just as you are. You don't have to make sure you're all bright and shiny when you approach Him. He wants the real you, even when you're upset or angry. God would rather you whine, complain, cry, curse, rant, and rave than withdraw. He can handle your passionate anger and your bitter fears and would rather you maintain relationship with Him than walk away, dismiss Him, and refuse to talk to Him. Indifference to God is worse than your anger, resentment, or frustration.

What if you're moody one day and happy the next? God still wants you to pray.

When you do something you know you shouldn't have? He still wants to talk to you.

Whatever you're going through, wherever you are, prayer can always be your priority.

It's time to start praying *before* you act, not after.

No matter what you're doing, *pray first*!

two

the place of prayer

———————

But when you pray, go into your
room, close the door and pray to
your Father, who is unseen.

—Matthew 6:6 NIV

Most mornings at home, I wake up while it's still dark outside. I've always been an early riser, and even when I change time zones or switch to daylight savings time, my body seems to awaken just before dawn. It usually doesn't matter how late I stayed up; just before sunrise, my body's natural alarm clock signals it's time to wake up. Over the years I've grown to love being a morning person, especially when it comes to prayer.

So I'll usually wake up while Tammy is still sleeping, just as sunlight begins creeping over the horizon out our window. I'll head downstairs and make a cup of coffee, then head to my office. There's a chair we've had forever, with a matching ottoman that's torn on one corner, which is known as "my spot." I'll shut the door behind me, because when I pray, it can get pretty loud.

First, I'll turn on some instrumental worship music and adjust the wireless speaker on the table beside my chair. I love hymns and praise songs with words, but during my morning prayer time, I don't want lyrics distracting me from listening to God and expressing my heart to Him. I want our conversation to be the priority.

Then I'll grab my Bible and spend some time listening to the Lord speak from His Word. Sometimes I'm drawn to a particular passage, and other times I go to a spot addressing a specific topic that's relevant to the day. I'll sip my coffee and read that day's scripture as slowly as possible, savoring it and letting it sink into my spirit. If a word or phrase jumps out at me from the passage, I'll meditate on it and see what the Holy Spirit might be telling me.

After I've read the Word and listened to God, I'll choose a guide or resource to help me focus my prayers. I have a drawer filled with file folders and loose papers that I've collected over the past four decades. Most of the time, they remain scattered across my desk rather than tucked in my prayer drawer because I use them so often. Some are stapled together, while others are getting dog-eared at the corners from using them so often. My notes, comments, and edits are scribbled in pen and pencil on most sheets, indicating an idea, reference, or action based on that particular guide's instruction.

Then I pray, using my selected guide or resource—just like the ones I'm sharing with you in this book—to facilitate my time with God. I keep pens and highlighters handy to jot down anything noteworthy, such as someone I feel compelled to continue praying for or an idea or point for that week's sermon. I move through the prayer time, always including a time of praise for all God is doing and worship for who He is. I'll lift up my needs and the needs of my family, close friends, our staff at church, and others in our Highlands family.

By the end of my prayer time, usually somewhere between thirty minutes and an hour, I'll have cranked up the praise-and-worship music, and there's a good chance I might be singing. Then I'll usually go grab another cup of coffee and head upstairs to shower and dress and get going.

Many mornings when I return to our bedroom, Tammy is up and in the midst of her own prayer time. She will be sitting in her special chair, reading her Bible or bowing her head. Sometimes she's whispering in conversation with the Father, and many times she already has a tissue in hand for the tears that inevitably come. Seeing her so intimately connected to God always moves me. I can only imagine how He feels when she—or any of us, really—open our hearts to Him.

Aprons and Prayer Shawls

I share these details with you not to brag or imply anyone should pray like we do, but simply to make two important points about prioritizing prayer. First, *where* you pray on a consistent basis is important. Like all the other details of communicating with someone, your setting matters. Where we pray is important and often facilitates our ability to focus on God without interruption or distraction. Jesus had special places to pray, and we need one too.

The second reason I describe our prayer places is to show you a little of the variety. While it's important to have a special prayer place, there's nothing necessarily special about the place itself—other than it's your meeting place with God. It doesn't have to be a dedicated room or private chapel. In fact, it doesn't even have to be a distinct physical place but could be one you take with you, as the ancient Jewish tradition reminds us.

When Jewish people prayed, they were either in the temple or beneath their prayer shawl. Known as a *tallit*, this woven covering was usually held above or over the heads of those wishing to pray. In the intimacy of this individual tent, the person could shut out distractions while also signaling to others that they were not to be disturbed. The tallit was considered part of the standard apparel for Jewish men, draped over the shoulders or around their cloak, which made it portable and instantly available. They always had a place to pray that was all their own.

Many people, both Jewish and Christian, continue to use prayer shawls today. John Wesley, the great eighteenth-century evangelist, once told how his mother, Susanna, used her apron as her prayer shawl. She would raise it over her face to block out the many distractions of her nineteen (yes, nineteen!) children.[1] Even with her large family clamoring for her attention, Mrs. Wesley found a way to pray daily and privately.

That's what having a place to pray is all about—consistency and intimacy.

Go to Your Room

The consistency and intimacy we need in prayer come from following the instructions Jesus gave His followers about prayer. Before He gave us the model of prayer we know as the Lord's Prayer, Jesus emphasized the importance of making prayer relational and personal, not public and conspicuous:

> "And when you pray, do not be like the hypocrites, for they love to pray standing in the synagogues and on the street corners to be seen by others. Truly I tell you, they have received their reward in full. But when you pray, go into your room, close the door and pray to your Father, who is unseen. Then your Father, who sees what is done in secret, will reward you." (Matthew 6:5–6 NIV)

The contrast here implies that the purpose of a private prayer room is to avoid the temptation that often accompanies public prayer: the desire to attract the admiring attention of others. We tend to think we need prayer rooms to insulate us from our lives' many interruptions, diversions, and distractions, but Jesus says having a private prayer place also reinforces humility. While you and I may not be tempted to pray loud, eloquent prayers in public so that others will think us amazing Christians, the need to keep our conversations with God to ourselves still matters.

The word translated as "room" in Jesus' instruction is from the Greek *tameion*, which refers to a storage chamber or secret room found in many Jewish households at that time. Such small spaces were practical for not only storing wine, linens, or other domestic items but also hiding valuables and money. Those who heard Jesus make this reference likely understood that He wasn't being literal but figurative. He wanted them to understand prayer is about connecting with God personally, not performing for others to see.

This principle still applies to us even if we're not praying publicly. Many people still take pride in performing for others in more subtle ways, wanting to be seen as someone admired and respected for their faith. The tendency to people-please causes some believers to work hard to be seen as a "good Christian."

This might come out in the way you casually mention what you're reading for your quiet time or making sure your coworkers know that you got up early to stop and pray at your church before clocking in at work. It might be making an effort to be obvious and noticeable when you pray before meals in restaurants. Anytime you shift the emphasis from focusing only on God to soliciting the approval and admiration of others, you run the risk of being like the hypocritical religious leaders of Jesus' day.

"Going to your room" and "praying in secret" happens inside your heart.

Make It Your Own

Nonetheless, retreating with God in the privacy of prayer can be reinforced by where you commune with Him logistically. Whether you use your apron as a prayer shawl like Mrs. Wesley or have a dedicated room in your home where you pray, the key is to go there daily to talk with the Lord. I believe it's the best way to start your day, but you decide the time that works best for you. The key is consistency in an environment conducive to connecting with God.

I've known people who use duck blinds, skateboard parks, beauty parlors, and cafeterias as their regular place of prayer. Others have a designated spot at home, their office, or their church. It could be a closet, a walk-in pantry, a corner of the basement, or a window seat in the attic. Again, the place should help you be alone with God in your heart.

Many people tell me they like their place of prayer to be comfortable but not so comfortable that they doze off. Some people have bulletin boards in their place of prayer where they can post pictures of family and loved ones they pray for regularly along with specific requests or notes to remind them of upcoming events requiring prayer. You might have a favorite verse written large to remind you of a particular promise related to a need or request.

Others use their phones in a similar way. They use apps, keep lists, listen to music, and organize pictures expressly for their prayer times. This method works well for people who travel frequently or don't feel drawn to return to the same location each day. Using their electronic version of a prayer shawl, they can spend time with God outside, in a coffee shop, on a plane, or during lunch.

Keep in mind, though, that you can have all kinds of tech assistance to facilitate your prayer time without actually praying. You can assemble dozens of books on prayer, scented candles, and praise-and-worship music and *still* not truly connect intimately with God in prayer. You can decorate a dedicated room in your home with beautiful pictures, a giant cross, and stained glass windows, but those details may mean nothing if you're not regularly going there to pray.

Where you pray is a matter of personal preference—as long as it helps you connect with God.

Get Creative

Having a regular place of prayer usually helps you prioritize prayer—until it doesn't. If you begin to feel bored or in a rut in your designated spot, then it's time to get creative and break up your routine. There are many ways to be creative in your prayer life, and we'll explore more of them in the chapters ahead, but a good way to jump-start your time with God is to try a new location.

It makes sense that changing where you meet God affects the quality of your time together. Early in our marriage, Tammy and I would have a date night because we knew we had to prioritize our time together in order to stay connected and keep our bond strong. Especially when our kids were little and I was focused on doing all that God called me to do, I looked forward to my regular weekly date with my wife—except for one thing: where to go. We were often both so tired that it became hard to be creative or spontaneous.

I'd ask, "Where do you want to go, honey?" and she would say, "Oh, anywhere is fine." Which meant I'd often choose the same restaurant where we usually ate because I knew the food would be good, prices were fair, and it was close to home. We enjoyed going there most weeks, and neither of us thought much about it—this restaurant became our default date-night place.

But after several months, when we realized we were going there almost every week, we knew it was definitely time for a change. By that time we had the menu memorized even though we typically ordered the same thing each visit. We knew the names of all the waitstaff and often the names of their spouses and kids. We sat at the same booth near the back corner because it was more private. While this familiarity was comfortable, it wasn't doing much to help us be closer and strengthen our relationship.

So we decided that we wouldn't go to the same spot twice for the next six months. We agreed to take turns deciding where we'd go and what we would do there. As a result, we ended up enjoying those new adventures much more because they forced us out of our comfort zone.

If your prayer life feels like it's on autopilot, maybe it's time to try different locations. Keep in mind that the emphasis is on spending alone time with God, so you might not want a place that's too crowded or noisy. Then again, that might be exactly where the Holy Spirit leads you to pray! Maybe go somewhere you normally don't. Try a place of worship you've never visited before. Pray for neighbors as you walk around the block. Volunteer at a shelter or food pantry and make it the center of your prayer time.

There's no right or wrong place as long as you pray—take God everywhere you go and keep the conversation going. Try to find the sweet spot in between having a consistent place and a creative catalyst for your prayer time. Just as going to the same restaurant for date night became monotonous and too easy, doing prayer in the same place for too long can contribute to spiritual stagnation. Don't be afraid to get creative and plan a special date with God!

Take It Outside

Perhaps one of the best places to connect with God is in the great outdoors. In a natural setting, you're sure to find details and vistas that cause you to marvel at their beauty—and the One who created them. Many people tell me they like praying on their porch, patio, or deck because it's never the same experience twice. Although their prayer place stays the same, the weather, lighting, and season create a unique environment every time.

Based on what we're told in the Bible about His time on earth, Jesus seemed to favor praying to His Father outdoors. In fact, nearly every reference to Jesus praying found in the Gospels mentions a natural setting. This makes sense in that Jesus didn't own a house or even have a regular place where He lived. As His ministry grew and He became more recognized, finding a

There's no right or wrong place as long as you pray—take God everywhere you go and keep the conversation going.

spot outdoors likely made it easier for Him to be alone without interruption. Here are a few of the key references to Jesus praying outside:

- "After he had dismissed them, he went up on a mountainside by himself to pray. Later that night, he was there alone." (Matthew 14:23 NIV)
- "Then Jesus went with his disciples to a place called Gethsemane, and he said to them, 'Sit here while I go over there and pray.'" (Matthew 26:36 NIV)
- "Very early in the morning, while it was still dark, Jesus got up, left the house and went off to a solitary place, where he prayed." (Mark 1:35 NIV)
- "After leaving them, he went up on a mountainside to pray." (Mark 6:46 NIV)
- "One of those days Jesus went out to a mountainside to pray, and spent the night praying to God." (Luke 6:12 NIV)

Notice that Christ seemed to favor the mountains, the wilderness or desolate places, and the garden of Gethsemane. I've been to the garden of Gethsemane in Israel, located in the valley between the Mount of Olives and the eastern side of the Holy City of Jerusalem. Many times I've wondered if Jesus liked to pray there because He could be so close to the city He loved and the people He loved.

If you want to pray like Jesus, consider finding a spot overlooking your neighborhood, community, or city where you can view its panorama. You don't have to go outside, though, to connect to

His heart for people, especially those lost and suffering. Wherever you pray, you can encounter the heart of God and be transformed. You will likely improve your ability to make prayer a priority if you have a designated spot, but the only prayer closet that's essential is within you.

Remember, a private place helps us pray—but pray wherever you are.

three

the plan of prayer

———

Lord, teach us to pray . . .

—Luke 11:1 NIV

If you want to prioritize prayer, you need a plan.

While this may seem obvious, my experience tells me that having a plan for your prayer time may be so obvious that it gets overlooked. When people tell me they struggle to pray, I'll ask them to describe their prayer process. Consistency is sometimes the issue, which may have to do with having a regular place and time to pray. More often, however, consistency and place are not the issues—it's what to do when they get there. They need a plan for their prayer time, to help them focus and go deeper than just a cursory communication.

Without a plan, we're likely to ramble in a stream-of-consciousness monologue. God knows our hearts, so ultimately the problem isn't lack of communication—it's the quality of the communication. When we don't have a prayer plan, we're much more prone to get in our own way, either rushing and rambling to check it off our lists or reciting and reading prayers without engaging our hearts.

Keeping It Real

Occasionally, someone will tell me that having a prayer plan hinders their spontaneity and ability to connect with God in various circumstances, moods, and settings. "Following a plan sounds like it will kill the romance and mystery of relating to God," one woman told me. "Real relationships don't require plans," she explained.

"Allow me to challenge that," I replied, confident we knew each other well enough for me to push back. "Do you and your husband ever discuss how to parent your children?"

"Yes, of course," she said, chuckling. "Usually when there's a problem."

"How about your finances? Do you two have conversations about budgets and bills on a regular basis?"

She nodded.

"What about your goals and dreams? Your fears and concerns for the future?"

"Sometimes. I see what you're saying," she said. "But those all come up based on our circumstances and contexts. Many times those issues will just come up in the course of everyday life."

"I agree—that's often the case when Tammy and I discuss things. But early in our marriage, we learned that it's helpful to have regular check-in times when we focus on the kids, our finances, vacations and big events coming up, our physical health, and the health of our marriage. We don't have big agendas—we simply want to connect and get on the same page. Our commitment to discuss our priorities makes sure we stay connected. Having a plan when you pray accomplishes the same thing."

Rather than undermining true connection and a deeper relationship, having a plan when you pray does just the opposite. It frees you up to stay focused on what matters most. It prevents you from overlooking or neglecting certain aspects of your relationship. Having a prayer plan will help you take your time with God seriously.

Prayer Protocol

Using a plan when you pray also provides a protocol for your connection time with God. In other words, a plan not only focuses your topics and methods of praying but also facilitates the tone and attitude of how you meet God. It shows an awareness of how important God is to you and how much you love communicating with Him.

Even though my kids know they can ask me anything, if they just barged into my office and directly asked for things without first acknowledging our relationship, I would feel disrespected. Instead of "Hey, I need some money!" they typically check in first and reconnect. Most times, they might knock on my door and look in. "Hi, Dad, how's your day going? Is now a good time to talk?" Similarly, we enter into our conversation with God by focusing on Him before ourselves. Our focus should be on relational connection, including the kind of respect and honor God deserves from us.

When we don't have a protocol in planning our time with Him each day, I wonder how God feels when we just start asking for things. Instead of showing honor and respect, instead of leading up to larger concerns, instead of focusing on our relationship, we often act like we're placing an order at the Heavenly Drive-Thru. "Uh, yeah, Lord, I'd really like You to heal my sprained ankle, my cousin's cancer, and that lady with bad arthritis at church. I need more money as well to pay all the bills that keep piling up. And You know I really want a promotion at work. Okay, thanks, God—that's it for now." If that's how you're praying, you might as well add a side of fries with that!

We don't begin conversations with friends this way, and we shouldn't begin our time with God this way either. It's thoughtless, rude, and disrespectful to the relationship. It reflects an attitude that God is just there for what He can do for you. Such discourtesy treats God not as your Abba Father but like a genie. Obviously, that's not who He is, and that's not how your relationship with Him should work.

Let the Lord know you recognize and acknowledge who He is and that you love Him simply for being your Father.

Prayer Freeze

Some people who struggle to know what to talk about with God may have experienced what I call "prayer freeze" at an early age. I remember being part of "prayer circles" when I was a child in Sunday school. Our teacher had us put our chairs in a circle, hold hands, and go around so that each person could pray. When you were finished praying, you were supposed to give a gentle squeeze to the next person to signal their turn.

As a shy kid I was already nervous about having to say anything in front of others, and now I had to include God. The unspoken rule was not to repeat what had already been prayed, so I would sit there dreading the inevitable squeeze, afraid that I would stutter, stammer, or say nothing at all. I felt the available list of items get smaller and smaller with each classmate who prayed. Sometimes, I just kept the circle moving with a squeeze-squeeze because I didn't know what to say. I wanted to pray to God but worried about how I'd sound to everyone else.

Other times when I knew I was supposed to pray, I learned prayers that made me wonder what I was actually saying. You know, like "Now I lay me down to sleep, I pray the Lord my soul to keep. If I should die before I wake, I pray the Lord my soul to take." I don't know about you, but that always seemed a little creepy to me, like any kid wants to think about dying right before bedtime.

Grace before meals wasn't much better. "God is great, God is good, now we thank Him for our food." My sister and I took turns trying to see who could say it faster, and the result was more like sound effects than prayers, much to our parents' disapproval. Again, not a great model for communicating with God.

No wonder I felt like I didn't know how to pray! Maybe you felt like that too. And it's not only kids wondering how we should pray. In fact, some of Jesus' disciples, who most likely learned traditional Jewish prayers growing up, overheard their Master praying and must have been stunned—because they asked Him to teach them to pray like that. "Once Jesus was in a certain place praying. As he finished, one of his disciples came to him and said, 'Lord, teach us to pray, just as John taught his disciples.' Jesus said, 'This is how you should pray . . .'" (Luke 11:1–2 NLT).

Clearly, the way Jesus prayed must have been different from the methods and prayers they had experienced growing up.

The Lord's Prayer . . . or the Lord's Outline?

In the Jewish culture of their time, these men probably learned traditional Jewish prayers that had been passed down from generation to generation, memorizing the words as they matured into adulthood. These would have included prayers to pray at different times, events, and holy days. But like so many things we're told we must learn, these prayers may have seemed disconnected from having an actual conversation with God.

They became set pieces tied to religion instead of open doors to relationship.

There's nothing wrong with praying such prayers—and we'll be looking at several of them in part 2—but the key is *how* and *why* you use them. Simply put, prayers should draw you closer to God. Prayers that are treated as a script, rote recital, or ancestral throwback don't facilitate a vibrant, communicative relationship between you and God.

That's likely one of the qualities the disciples noted when they overheard Jesus praying. He addressed God as His Father in a tone that was probably personal, conversational, and intimate. Some of the words and phrases they heard Jesus use may have been similar to the Jewish prayers they already knew, but *how* Jesus used them to address His Father must have seemed different.

In part 2 we'll carefully explore the model of prayer Jesus taught His followers, but for now let's consider that He didn't teach them a specific prayer to pray but a *plan* for prayer. What if Christ was not passing along special poetic phrases to be recited as an incantation to open heaven's gate? What if what we now call the Lord's Prayer is actually what we should be using as the Lord's Outline?

There are two gospel accounts of Jesus teaching this prayer model. In Luke, one of the disciples specifically asked Jesus to teach them how to pray. In Matthew, the Lord's instruction on how to pray is included as part of the Sermon on the Mount: "Now when Jesus saw the crowds, he went up on a mountainside and sat down. His disciples came to him, and he began to teach them" (Matthew 5:1–2 NIV).

Simply put, prayers should draw you closer to God. Prayers that are treated as a script, rote recital, or ancestral throwback don't facilitate a vibrant, communicative relationship between you and God.

In both gospel accounts, Jesus wanted to instruct His followers, to teach them how to connect with God as their Father as opposed to reciting a memorized set of traditional words. Rather than going through the motions, Jesus stressed the importance of examining one's motives for praying—and frequently called out the Pharisees for focusing on external appearances rather than their internal connection to God. In one confrontation with them, Jesus called them hypocrites and said, "You nullify the word of God for the sake of your tradition. . . . Isaiah was right when he prophesied about you:

> "These people honor me with their lips,
>> but their hearts are far from me.
> They worship me in vain;
>> their teachings are merely human rules."

(Matthew 15:6–9 NIV)

By referencing Isaiah (29:13), Jesus indicated that this tendency to give God lit service while remaining far from Him was nothing new. This was the radical aspect of the prayer Jesus taught His followers to use—it provided a plan for maintaining an intimate relationship with the living God.

Don't Perform Your Piety

Based on how Jesus prefaced His model of prayer in Matthew, some people had apparently been using prayer as a status symbol of their righteousness. "Be careful not to practice your righteousness in front of others to be seen by them," Jesus warned. "If you do, you will have no reward from your Father in heaven" (Matthew 6:1 NIV). Notice that He didn't tell them not to pray in public. Rather, Jesus cautioned them not to pray in public *in order to impress others with their righteousness.* To drive home His point, Jesus continued:

> "And when you pray, do not be like the hypocrites, for they love to pray standing in the synagogues and on the street corners to be seen by others. Truly I tell you, they have received their reward in full. But when you pray, go into your room, close the door and pray to your Father, who is unseen. Then your Father, who sees what is done in secret, will reward you. And when you pray, do not keep on babbling like pagans, for they think they will be heard because of their many words. Do not be like them, for your Father knows what you need before you ask him." (Matthew 6:5–8 NIV)

Two points stand out in this elaboration. First, don't pray as a performance of your piety in hopes that others will notice how spiritual you are. That's what hypocrites do. They're not praying to connect with God—they're praying to appear better than others. Instead, keep your prayers quiet and private, personal between you and God. Second, don't assume that God rewards you by your word count. Jesus cited the way pagans kept babbling in hopes that using words would be more effective. We don't need to worry about quantity as much as quality when we pray; our heavenly

Father already knows our needs without our articulating them. Again, prayer is not about performance or "doing enough." Prayer is about connecting with God.

Jesus then taught His followers the perfect plan for how to pray. Based on how He prefaced this model, I believe being deliberate about a plan for prayer matters because it forces you to consider why you're praying. Every plan has a purpose. The hypocrites and pagans didn't need to follow a plan when praying because they weren't pursuing a relational conversation with God. One group just wanted to look holy and morally superior, while the other wanted to keep talking in hopes they'd get what they requested.

Putting a prayer plan in place helps you stay focused on the real purpose of prayer: knowing and staying close with God.

Creative Planning

Think of your prayer plan as a compass to help you navigate your relationship with the Lord. The plan you choose will vary depending on where you want to go in knowing Him each time you pray. You may want to focus on His grace and mercy, so you use the Psalms as a guide for exploring this aspect of God's character. Perhaps you want to pray on behalf of loved ones who are struggling, so you make prayers of intercession (prayers on behalf of or for the needs of others) your focus. You might be struggling with ongoing temptation, so you rely on spiritual warfare prayers based on relevant passages of Scripture. Choosing a plan for your prayer time can help you clarify your most pressing concerns before you turn them over to God.

Knowing when to change your plan and shift focus is also important. Plans often reinforce your consistency but can become stale over time. You don't want your plan to become a rut or a shallow way to pray without connecting with God on a deep, personal level. Creativity and variety in your plans can help keep your relationship engaging and dynamic. Including music, using different devotionals and Bible commentaries, and using various formats often keep your prayer plans fresh and exciting. The more plans you have on hand, the more options you have in how you spend time with God.

I've spent my life collecting plans for prayer. Basically, the result is everything I'm sharing with you in these pages. Beginning with the prayer-starters I learned from some of my pastors and mentors, I've accumulated a dozen pages with various prayer plans, lists, verses, and prompts. Some are handwritten, others are old-fashioned copies, and a few are handouts given to me. If there's been a secret to sustaining my relationship with God, it's using these plans to seek Him, know Him, worship and praise Him, and love Him. I've always loved teaching prayer, not because I've mastered it, but because I'm determined to know God and grow our relationship as much as possible in this lifetime.

Prayer plans aren't only for your individual prayer times, of course. Some of my favorite memories of pastoring are the prayer services I've been privileged to experience. Early in my ministry career when I was a youth pastor, I led the Wednesday night service at our church. To help prepare for that service, I would invite the entire youth group to my house on Tuesday evenings to pray. Usually, at least a hundred or so kids would show up, raiding my fridge and piling on cushions along the floor. They would all laugh and joke around until it was time to pray and get serious. Pulling from my own collection, I'd make copies to pass out to guide our time.

Those handouts eventually became the curated booklet we now use at Highlands entitled—you guessed it—"Pray First." And that booklet has been expanded into the book you're now holding. There's nothing magical about the models and methods of prayer that I love to share with others. But I believe having a plan when you pray can be a conduit for the supernatural connection between you and God.

Don't just pray first—*plan* to pray first!

four

the power of prayer

———

There has never been a spiritual
awakening in any country or locality
that did not begin in united prayer.

—A. T. Pierson

"Have you seen this?"

I smacked that morning's local newspaper on the conference
table, harder than I intended but nonetheless pleased with its
loud impact. The dozen members of our core team stared back at
me, well aware this wasn't how I usually started our weekly staff
meetings at Highlands.

"Is that about the crime rate here in Birmingham?" one of my team members asked. "That's crazy, isn't it?"

"It's more than crazy," I said. "It's *unacceptable*."

I quickly summarized the front-page story, based on an in-depth article in the latest *Forbes* magazine at the time.[2] According to their findings, Birmingham ranked as one of the most dangerous cities in America, coming in fifth based on the city's double-digit violent crime rate. Although overall crime was lower than it had been in the previous decade, the 1990s, the escalation in certain parts of our home city stunned us. As my righteous anger cooled to a manageable simmer, I was grateful that our team shared my indignation.

"We have to pray," I concluded after we had spent a few minutes brainstorming ways our church could respond to help this dire situation. "We need to get every church in the area involved and start prayer walking through these neighborhoods. We need to go to battle and ask God to make Birmingham safer."

The consequence of that conversation was the launch of Prayer Force United—a citywide, community-based initiative for people to gather, in conjunction with law enforcement and city officials, and prayer-walk through areas with the highest crime rates. Our goal became to gather once a month in an area selected by the city police leaders and walk through streets, parks, and neighborhoods praying together. We prayed not only for the darkness to be lifted in these locations but for local officials and law enforcement to be given wisdom, protection, and guidance on how best to deter crime in Birmingham.

Dramatic improvement occurred within a matter of months.

By the end of that year, the crime rate in the city of Birmingham had dropped to its lowest since 1966. The police force partnered with us and provided even more incredible service. They recognized the need and respected our intentions, with many of them joining us in prayer when possible.

Prayer prevailed when nothing else had worked.

Keys to Powerful Prayer

The power of prayer accomplished what many said could not be done in our city. But if you've ever experienced the power of God unleashed through prayer, then you know nothing is impossible—because the most powerful force on earth is not nuclear, atomic, military-based, or government-led. The most powerful force on earth is God's power in answer to the prayers of His people.

We see its power today just as the followers of Jesus saw it in the early church. One of the first prayer gatherings of the early church can be found in Acts 4. At this prayer gathering, Peter and John were reporting back to the community of believers after going before the Sanhedrin, the group of Jewish leaders made up of Pharisees, Sadducees, and temple priests.

They had been called to testify before these powerful leaders because of the encounter Peter and John had with a lame beggar outside the temple gates the day before. Crippled since birth, the man had asked the two disciples for money, to which Peter replied, "Silver or gold I do not have, but what I do have I give you. In the name of Jesus Christ of Nazareth, walk" (Acts 3:6 NIV). As Peter

The most powerful
force on earth is
not nuclear, atomic,
military-based, or
government-led. The
most powerful force
on earth is God's
power in answer
to the prayers
of His people.

helped him stand, "instantly the man's feet and ankles became strong. He jumped to his feet and began to walk" (vv. 7–8 NIV).

When the man began walking and jumping and praising God along the temple courts, people recognized him as the lame beggar they had seen beside the gate for years, possibly decades. Soon a crowd gathered, eager to question the man and discover the source of his miraculous healing. Perhaps intimidated by the growing throng of people, the man rushed back to Peter and John, who seized the opportunity to share the gospel of Jesus Christ.

They preached until evening, when they were arrested, but not before "the number of men who believed grew to about five thousand" (Acts 4:4 NIV). Keep in mind, this resulted from Peter and John healing that one lame man, whose testimony couldn't be suppressed. Unfortunately, the religious and political leaders found this joyous result threatening. Good news for God's kingdom caused them to fear for their own shrinking power base.

Undaunted when brought before the Jewish council of leaders the following day, Peter and John refused to back down from preaching about Jesus and demonstrating the power of the Holy Spirit. Their blunt testimony put the Sanhedrin members in a quandary. "After further threats they let them go. They could not decide how to punish them, because all the people were praising God for what had happened" (Acts 4:21 NIV).

Now comes the part of the story that intrigues me—one of the very first prayer meetings described in the New Testament. Rather than hiding or complaining or whining about how mistreated and misunderstood they had been for doing a good deed, Peter and John went to their power source in prayer to recharge:

> On their release, Peter and John went back to their own people and reported all that the chief priests and the elders had said to them. When they heard this, they raised their voices together in prayer to God. "Sovereign Lord," they said, "you made the heavens and the earth and the sea, and everything in them. You spoke by the Holy Spirit through the mouth of your servant, our father David:
>
>> "'Why do the nations rage
>>   and the peoples plot in vain?
>> The kings of the earth rise up
>>   and the rulers band together
>> against the Lord
>>   and against his anointed one.'
>
> Indeed Herod and Pontius Pilate met together with the Gentiles and the people of Israel in this city to conspire against your holy servant Jesus, whom you anointed. They did what your power and will had decided beforehand should happen. Now, Lord, consider their threats and enable your servants to speak your word with great boldness. Stretch out your hand to heal and perform signs and wonders through the name of your holy servant Jesus."
>
> After they prayed, the place where they were meeting was

shaken. And they were all filled with the Holy Spirit and spoke the word of God boldly. (Acts 4:23–31 NIV)

Their example demonstrates three important points about powerful prayers that still apply to us. Powerful prayers are unified, scriptural, and bold. Let's explore each of these and how we can experience the same miraculous, dynamic power of God when we pray.

Raising Voices Together: Unified Prayer

I don't know about you, but this prayer meeting wasn't like the ones I grew up attending. This community of believers gathered together, heard Peter and John's report, and "raised their voices together in prayer" (Acts 4:24 NIV). They didn't wait on Peter and John to pray for them all. They didn't appoint one person to pray while everyone else bowed their heads and murmured, "Uh huh, yes, Lord." They didn't whisper to themselves. And they didn't take a shotgun approach with everyone praying through their own variety of requests.

No, they raised their voices together in prayer!

They knew through the power of God's Spirit that their prayers had the greatest impact when they prayed in one accord. Powerful prayers are unified. Why? Because God longs for His people to come together in prayer: "If *my people*, who are called by my name, will humble themselves and pray and seek my face and turn from their wicked ways, then I will *hear* from heaven, and

I will *forgive* their sin and will *heal* their land" (2 Chronicles 7:14 NIV, emphasis added). Notice what happens when God's people humble themselves, seek His face, and turn away from sin. God hears their prayers, forgives their sins, and heals their land.

With all that's happening in our world today at every level, this promise seems more urgent perhaps than ever before. People are looking for solutions that only God can provide. But it begins when we come together with our hearts aligned by the same purpose, to pray in unity. Jesus reinforced this truth when He told His followers:

> "Truly I tell you, whatever you bind on earth will be bound in heaven, and whatever you loose on earth will be loosed in heaven. Again, truly I tell you that if two of you on earth agree about anything they ask for, it will be done for them by my Father in heaven. For where two or three gather in my name, there am I with them." (Matthew 18:18–20 NIV)

This aspect of prayer remains integral to everything we do at Church of the Highlands. When God called me to start a new church, I knew immediately that it could only happen through His power. And I knew that His power could be accessed through the unified prayers of His people. So before we ever moved from Louisiana and our home church in Baton Rouge to Alabama, we prayed and fasted in unity.

We were so concerned about building this new church through God's efforts and not our own that we gathered together for twenty-one days. Each evening at six o'clock, more than thirty people would show up at my house. We would pray in our living room, gathered around the coffee table piled high with sixty thousand postcard mailers announcing our new church. We knew then that we were part of something that only God could do.

Once we started Church of the Highlands, we immediately began Saturday Prayers, asking people to come together and pray for what God wanted to do through us. We bathed every aspect of our services, our communities, and our people with unified prayer. Our commitment to prayer remains just as strong today. We have more than a thousand people on our prayer teams, praying before, during, and after each service, event, conference, and endeavor we start. Prayer is the lifeblood of our church, and we want it flowing in the same direction—toward God.

Praying the Promises: Scriptural Prayer

We also focus on praying the promises of God directly from Scripture based on the example of those attending that prayer meeting in the early church: "You spoke by the Holy Spirit through the mouth of your servant, our father David: 'Why do the nations rage and the peoples plot in vain?'" (Acts 4:25 NIV). Notice how they described the motivation behind praying God's Word back to Him—that the Holy Spirit wrote the Bible. Someone in their group, or perhaps everyone in their group, thought of this passage from Psalm 2, which fit their scenario perfectly.

How does quoting the Bible back to God infuse power in our prayers? By turning to His promises for our particular needs, we glorify Him. His Word assures us, "For all of God's promises have been fulfilled in Christ with a resounding 'Yes!' And through Christ, our 'Amen' (which means 'Yes') ascends to God for his glory" (2 Corinthians 1:20 NLT). All of God's promises—and the Bible contains about four thousand of them—have been fulfilled in Christ. They are already completed. When we claim them and echo our "amens," we praise God for His glory.

If you've ever heard me pray, then you've probably heard me quote Scripture in my prayer. I love trusting God's promises and resting in the peace and confidence of knowing He always fulfills His Word. Sometimes I hear people pray in a way that seems so wishy-washy: "Okay, Lord, whatever You want, Your will be done. If You can help my kids stay out of trouble and not stray from You, that would be great."

Those kinds of prayers seem lacking in the certainty we have in the promises found in the Bible. When praying for my family, I'm not doing it half-heartedly with an anything-goes attitude. I'm believing that based on Joshua 24:15—my kids and grandkids *will* serve the Lord! After someone broke into our first apartment and robbed us, Tammy and I prayed Psalm 144—there will be no breaching of our walls and no going into captivity.

Jesus said, "Everyone who hears these words of mine and puts them into practice is like a wise man who built his house on the rock" (Matthew 7:24 NIV). When we pray God's promises, we're putting Jesus' words into practice, laying a firm foundation for our lives. So anytime I have a problem, big or small, I find a promise to pray. Praying God's promises exercises my faith and strengthens it at the same time.

This isn't a "name it and claim it" formula or "blab it and grab it" gimmick. When you pray the promises of God, you're focusing on God's power and limitless resources rather than the problem or your own very limited ability to solve it. Your heavenly Father is bigger than any situation you'll encounter, no matter how painful or scary or uncertain it may seem in the moment.

Whatever you're going through, find a verse for the situation and trust God for the result. Pray His promises and trust in His power to be revealed. For example, here are a few of my favorites to get you started. (All scriptures are taken from the NIV.)

- **Challenges**—1 John 4:4; Luke 10:19; Romans 8:37 ("We are more than conquerors.")
- **Finances**—Psalm 1:1–3; Philippians 4:19 ("My God will meet all your needs.")
- **Troubling emotions**—Psalm 27:1 ("The LORD is my light and my salvation—whom shall I fear?")
- **Health**—Psalm 103:2–3 ("Praise the LORD . . . [who] heals all your diseases.")
- **Confidence**—2 Corinthians 3:6 ("He has made us competent.")
- **Safety**—Psalm 121:8 ("The LORD will watch over your coming and going.")
- **Even the dentist!**—Psalm 81:10 ("Open wide your mouth and I will fill it." Okay, maybe that's not what this verse is talking about!)

With Hearts Undaunted: Bold Prayer

Powerful prayers are unified, they draw on God's promises, and finally, they demonstrate *boldness*. Notice that the way Peter and John acted certainly displayed this quality, but boldness is also something their group requested going forward. They didn't want to rest on past events but wanted to be conduits of God's power: "Now, Lord, consider their threats and enable your servants to speak your word with great boldness. Stretch out your hand to heal and perform signs and wonders through the name of your holy servant Jesus" (Acts 4:29–30 NIV).

Apparently, God answered this prayer right away: "After they prayed, the place where they were meeting was shaken. And they were all filled with the Holy Spirit and spoke the word of God boldly" (Acts 4:31 NIV). When we request this same kind of boldness, it indicates how much we're willing to rely on God—and to be used by Him. We demonstrate that our emotions and circumstances cannot get in the way of God's Spirit.

God seems to delight in answering our request for His boldness. We're told, "The effective, fervent prayer of a righteous man avails much" (James 5:16 NKJV). The two adjectives here—*effective* and *fervent*—are actually one word in the Greek, *energeo*. As you might suspect, it's connected with the idea of energy, especially the kind that's red-hot, on fire, and boiling over. This is the kind of boldness in prayer that reflects God's mighty power.

No wonder then that the devil likes weak prayers—ones that are passive and detached, distracted and disengaged. But I'm convinced we insult God with timid prayers and tepid faith. If our prayers are possible for us to fulfill, then they disrespect God because we don't really require His divine intervention or supernatural power. God honors *bold prayers* because bold prayers *honor God.*

When we pray with the same passionate commitment as those first believers described in the New Testament, we transcend the limitations imposed on us by others—and ourselves. We rely on God

God honors *bold prayers* because bold prayers *honor God.*

and trust in His ability to do what we can never do for ourselves. To see God's power unleashed, pray in unity, pray the promises of Scripture, and pray boldly.

And no matter what you're doing—*pray first!*

five

the persons of prayer

——————

The whole threefold life of the three-personal Being is actually going on in that ordinary little bedroom where an ordinary man is saying his prayers.

—C. S. Lewis

My attorney has become someone I trust implicitly. He's a personal friend who is looking out for me and intercedes when needed. I know he understands the law thoroughly should I seek his counsel. Having him in my life allows me to relax and experience more peace. I know that I can rest easy because he is my advocate, championing my cause no matter what situation may arise.

Someone else I appreciate even more is my father. The older I've gotten, the more I recognize what an incredible blessing my dad remains in my life. Although he's in heaven now, I think of him almost every day and thank God for the lessons my earthly father taught me about my heavenly Father. My dad was there for me throughout his life, demonstrating by example and generously giving me his time and attention. I know my father loved me because he told me so whenever we were together. More than that, he showed me by the way he talked with me and always hugged me. While I've been blessed with other father figures in my life, no one has loved me the way my dad did.

As I grow older, I also appreciate my closest friend more. I've known him for years and years. We've done life together, raised our kids together, ministered and served together, vacationed and relaxed together, suffered and hurt together, and grown closer throughout the process. He has been there for me at the lowest points of my life, when I was so depressed and didn't know what to do. He prays for me and provides wise counsel when I need another perspective to assess a situation. He's closer than a brother and sharpens me as iron sharpens iron.

I tell you about these three persons—my attorney, my father, and my best friend—in order to contrast the unique ways we relate to one another. Despite how much I love and enjoy my friends, there's no one who fills my heart the way my dad does. And as much as I appreciate all the wisdom and experience my father shared with me, I still rely on my attorney when I face a legal situation or need insight into the law. My attorney has a great sense of humor and we have a lot in common, but he's not the kind of friend who has refrigerator privileges or laughs at my bad jokes.

As you may have guessed by now, I'm also describing these three kinds of relationships to illustrate the unique way we relate to the three persons of the Godhead—Father, Son, and Holy Spirit. Each has a special and distinct relational dynamic. Understanding each holy person in the Trinity not only increases your grasp of who God is—it also helps you pray.

Amazing Grace of Jesus

As we've seen, prayer is not about specific words or methods. Words and methods are means to an end. Prayer is about communication in the personal relationship you have with the living God.

In order to be truly and fully relational, prayer revolves around intimacy with the vastness of who God is as three persons in One, also called the Trinity. Each person in the Godhead has a different, distinct role. And one of the best and most concise descriptions of their unique roles can be found in Paul's benediction in his second letter to the community of believers at Corinth. He concluded with a blessing encompassing all three persons of God: "The amazing grace of the Master, Jesus Christ, the extravagant love of God, the intimate friendship of the Holy Spirit, be with all of you" (2 Corinthians 13:14 THE MESSAGE).

Notice that there's nothing random about who Paul mentioned first here and the role of this person. The amazing grace of Jesus is mentioned first for two reasons. First and foremost, Jesus is the mediator, the intercessor, between us and God. You've probably noticed that we pray to God in Jesus' name. Christ connects us to our Father. Through Jesus we have access to Almighty God. Technically, we don't pray *to* Jesus—we pray *through* His intercession to the Father on our behalf.

How does this work? Jesus intercedes and expresses our prayers through His unique viewpoint—He is the only member of the Trinity to live as a human being on earth. Therefore, Christ knows firsthand just how challenging and painful our lives can be. "For we do not have a high priest who is unable to empathize with our weaknesses, but we have one who has been tempted in every way, just as we are—yet he did not sin. Let us then approach God's throne of grace with confidence, so that we may receive mercy and find grace to help us in our time of need" (Hebrews 4:15–16 NIV).

Think about this for a moment. Jesus has been tempted in every way and experienced the full spectrum of what it means to be human. He knows the depths of our thoughts, feelings, and longings. I love the way other Bible versions render this passage. The American Standard Version describes that Jesus knows what it's like to be "touched with the feeling of our infirmities" (Hebrews 4:15). In *The Message* Eugene Peterson paraphrased this truth so aptly: "We don't have a priest who is out of touch with our reality. He's been through weakness and testing, experienced it all—all but the sin. So let's walk right up to him and get what he is so ready to give. Take the mercy, accept the help" (Hebrews 4:15–16 THE MESSAGE).

Sometimes I imagine that as I'm praying, Jesus immediately conveys my needs and requests directly to God the Father: "Dad, I'm here on behalf of Chris. He's really struggling right now. I know how hard it is because I've felt the same way. Those circumstances are tough and emotions can get so intense. Chris needs our help right away." He's the expert on fulfilling the law, just like my earthly attorney, but on a spiritual, eternal level. Jesus pleads my case before the Father just as my attorney might plead for me in a court of law.

Just imagine Jesus praying specifically for you next time you're praying. Imagine Him turning to God the Father, both His Father and your Abba Father, and explaining what you need and why you need it. If it helps, picture Jesus as your attorney, making your case before the ultimate judge—not a stern, heartless judge but one who cares and wants what's best for you.

Another reason Paul mentioned Jesus first is because Christ is the member of the Godhead who made it possible for us to relate to God as His children, as co-heirs with His Son, Jesus. We access God through the amazing grace of Jesus. Without it, we are unable to approach God due to our sinfulness.

The price Jesus paid at the cross makes it possible for us to speak with God in all three persons. Jesus is not only our intercessor and mediator—He is our Savior, the One who overcame sin and death so that we might know God intimately and enjoy eternal life with Him in heaven. Through Jesus we receive the gift of grace and by grace we are saved (Ephesians 2:8–9 NIV).

In the Old Testament, before people would enter the tabernacle, they left a sacrifice on the brazen altar, temporarily cleansing them so that they could enter and encounter Holy God. Through His death on the cross, Jesus made this sacrifice for us once and for all, giving us immediate and eternal access to God's holy presence wherever we are. Thanks to Christ, nothing can separate us from God now!

Lavish Love of the Father

Focusing on the person of Jesus Christ, God the Son, is the first foundation of relational connection in prayer. Jesus made the way for us to experience "the extravagant love of God," the second phrase in Paul's benediction in 2 Corinthians 13:14 (THE MESSAGE). The Father's lavish love for us was the catalyst for sending Jesus to earth as a man to free us of the debt of sin that we could never permanently pay ourselves. "For God so loved the world that he gave his one and only Son, that whoever believes in him shall not perish but have eternal life" (John 3:16 NIV).

Unfortunately, our associations with our earthly fathers can pollute our view of our heavenly Father. And our view of God determines our relationship with God. We need a right view of God the Father to have a right relationship with Him.

I spoke to someone recently who told me they could not call God their Father because of the pain and trauma they had experienced with their earthly father. "I just work around it," they said. "I can pray to Him as Almighty God and Lord and Master, but Father just doesn't work for me."

As I explained to my friend, though, *not* knowing God as Father won't work for anyone who longs to connect, love, and worship Him. After describing the grace of God found in Christ, Paul wrote, "For this reason I kneel before the Father, from whom every family in heaven and on earth derives its name" (Ephesians 3:14–15 NIV). It's worth noting, as many translations and commentaries mention, that the word "family" here is *patria*, the Greek word derived from *pater*, meaning "father." As part of God's family, we look to Him as our Father, our Creator.

Viewing God as our Father results in approaching Him with our worship. This attitude is one of submission, reverence, honor, and respect. In the Old Testament, we're often told to "fear the Lord," which is another way of saying "worship Him." *Worship* and *fear* are often used interchangeably in referring to our posture before our heavenly Father.

Using *fear* in reference to worship doesn't mean to cower, cringe, or be afraid of God. This kind of fear is more like awe and recognition of God's greatness. In a healthy family, children both love and respect their father. They receive his love and protection as well as recognize his authority and power. In the Hebrew culture, children would almost always kneel in the presence of their father and wait for him to bless them. Worshiping God as our Father is quite similar.

This is the posture of our hearts before God as our heavenly Father. And perhaps nothing expresses this kind of worshipful attitude as beautifully as Psalm 103, which describes God's attributes so clearly and poetically:

> The LORD is compassionate and gracious,
>> slow to anger, abounding in love.
> He will not always accuse,
>> nor will he harbor his anger forever;
> he does not treat us as our sins deserve
>> or repay us according to our iniquities.
> For as high as the heavens are above the earth,
>> so great is his love for those who fear him;
> as far as the east is from the west,
>> so far has he removed our transgressions
>> from us.
> As a father has compassion on his children,
>> so the LORD has compassion on those who
>> fear him.

(Psalm 103:8–13 NIV)

Another passage that illustrates the lavish love of God the Father is found in the parable Jesus told about a prodigal son (Luke 15:11–32). You may recall that the younger of two sons audaciously asked his father for his inheritance early, basically insulting his dad and severing their relationship. After squandering the money on pleasure and luxury, the son ended up feeding pigs to survive. Then, coming to his senses, the young man realized that even the lowliest of servants in his father's house received better treatment than he was experiencing, so he decided to return home and beg forgiveness.

Expecting to be punished and humiliated, which would have been justifiable considering what he had done, the son returned home hoping to be treated as well as his father's servants. "But while he was still a long way off, his father saw him and was filled with compassion for him; he ran to his son, threw his arms around him and kissed him" (Luke 15:20 NIV). Rather than treat his wayward son like a servant, the father showed his lavish love by killing the fatted calf and throwing a huge homecoming party.

If you don't know God as the Father willing to run to you, throw His arms around you, and kiss your cheek to welcome you home, then you're missing out on who He really is. He does this because He simply loves you, not because of what you do or don't do. Remember, the prodigal son messed up in about the worst, most embarrassing ways for his culture, and his father still welcomed him home with open arms. God the Father loves you lavishly and wants you to know Him.

Faithful Friendship of the Holy Spirit

After you connect with the amazing grace of Jesus and the lavish love of the Father, then you're ready to experience the intimate friendship of the Holy Spirit. So many people struggle with this person of the Trinity and freak out about connecting with the "Holy Ghost." They act like they're going to a Halloween party instead of a prayer meeting!

Rather than be afraid, skeptical, or tentative about the Holy Spirit, recognize that He is the person who indwells you with God's presence all the time. You pray to Jesus and to the Father,

If you don't know
God as the Father
willing to run to
you, throw His
arms around you,
and kiss your cheek
to welcome you
home, then you're
missing out on
who He really is.

but the Spirit goes with you. He's the One telling you, "Okay, let's go live life!" The Holy Spirit was sent from heaven to be here on earth with you and in you. He's the friend accompanying you every step of every day.

Focusing on communion with the Holy Spirit is like being with your best friend all day long. Consequently, it's essential to cultivate and develop a friendship with Him. As you get to know Him more and more, you can pray from the bond of friendship and fellowship you experience. The word translated as Holy Spirit is usually *parakletos*, Greek that literally means "one called to be by one's side."

He is your friend, advocate, champion, guardian, and an additional kind of intercessor. He is the gift you receive when you accept God's grace and choose to follow Jesus. In fact, when preparing His followers for the arrival of this unique person, Jesus described Him like this: "But the Comforter, which is the Holy Ghost, whom the Father will send in my name, he shall teach you all things, and bring all things to your remembrance, whatsoever I have said unto you" (John 14:26 KJV).

The Holy Spirit fortifies you when you're struggling and gives you the power to resist temptation. He also intercedes on your behalf when you don't know what or how to pray. The Spirit knows you better than you know yourself. Paul wrote, "In the same way, the Spirit helps us in our weakness. We do not know what we ought to pray for, but the Spirit himself intercedes for us through wordless groans. And he who searches our hearts knows the mind of the Spirit, because the Spirit intercedes for God's people in accordance with the will of God" (Romans 8:26–27 NIV).

As if getting to know any one of the three persons of God is not incredible enough, we are blessed to relate to God as the Trinity. We come to Him through the grace and intercession of Jesus Christ, the Son. We worship God the Father and bask in His lavish love. We receive the Holy Spirit and experience the intimacy of friendship with a comforter, teacher, champion, and guardian. Each person offers different ways of knowing and experiencing God. If you want to strengthen your faith and know the Lord more intimately, then you must pray accordingly.

Pray first, and pray to the Three-in-One!

We come to Him through the grace and intercession of Jesus Christ, the Son. We worship God the Father and bask in His lavish love. We receive the Holy Spirit and experience the intimacy of friendship with a comforter, teacher, champion, and guardian.

part two

Prayer Models and How to Use Them

There is a mighty lot of difference
between saying prayers and praying.

—John G. Lake

six

the prayer of Jesus

———

For Yours is the kingdom and the
power and the glory forever.

—Matthew 6:13 NKJV

I'll never forget when my understanding of prayer
changed forever.

I was a sophomore in high school, fifteen years old and newly
saved, when my pastor, Larry Stockstill, taught on the Lord's
Prayer. Pastor Larry was passionate about prayer—to the point
that I half-expected him to preach on the power of prayer any
given Sunday. He even made sure we had prayer in the name of
our church: Bethany World Prayer Center.

But hearing him teach on prayer this time was different.

It was the first time I realized that the Lord's Prayer wasn't just a prayer—it was an *outline* for prayer. My mind was blown! I thought you were just supposed to memorize the Lord's Prayer and recite it whenever it was time to pray. And at that particular age and stage, the twenty-one seconds it took for me to say the Lord's Prayer was just about how long I spent in prayer. The main reason I didn't pray longer was that I didn't know what to say. So, like most of my friends and many of the Christians I knew, I would simply recite the Lord's Prayer, give God a few requests, and call it a day.

Learning to consider the Lord's Prayer as an outline, a model for prayer, remains one of the greatest discoveries in my entire Christian life to date. I hope this discovery can have the same impact on you.

When His disciples asked Him to teach them to pray, Jesus used a technique that many rabbis used—teaching God's truth by providing an outline drawn from the Scriptures. The disciples already knew how to pray based on their upbringing. They had learned traditional prayers that most Jewish males memorized as part of their upbringing.

But when they saw and heard Jesus pray, they were stunned. He wasn't praying as they had been taught, so they asked their Master to teach them to do it His way. So that's exactly what Jesus did—He gave them the gift of an outline for how to talk to the Father. It changed everything for the disciples that day, and it changed everything for me too.

Now I hope it changes the way you understand the Lord's Prayer—and perhaps all prayers!

Our Father in Heaven: Respect and Intimacy

As we discussed in chapter 3, having a deliberate plan in place when you pray goes a long way toward deepening your relationship with God. Rather than stifling your connection, a prayer plan facilitates staying focused and going deeper. The primary components of prayer planning are model prayers. These are not scripted prayers to be read verbatim but simply outlines, templates, and blueprints that help you include the major elements of prayer such as praise and worship, confession, petition, and intercession.

While we'll explore several distinct models found in the Bible, the best starting point is the prayer outline Jesus Himself gave us. It's the model prayer of all model prayers. In response to their request, Jesus instructed His followers to pray like this:

> "Our Father in heaven,
> Hallowed be Your name.
> Your kingdom come.
> Your will be done
> On earth as it is in heaven.
> Give us this day our daily bread.

And forgive us our debts,

As we forgive our debtors.

And do not lead us into temptation,

But deliver us from the evil one.

For Yours is the kingdom and the power

and the glory forever. Amen."

(Matthew 6:9–13 NKJV)

It's important to realize that Jesus wasn't teaching us words to memorize but rather how to connect with our Father. With this relational goal in mind, Christ gave us an outline with seven distinct aspects of prayer. Similar to rabbinical teaching of the day that followed specific outlines, Jesus concisely demonstrated elements for us to explore and expand upon as we pray.

A logical starting point when teaching others how to communicate is to focus on their audience, the person being addressed—and that's exactly how Jesus began: "Our Father in heaven . . ." It's difficult to grasp how radical it was for His disciples to hear that they—and we—should connect with God relationally. And not just relationally—we should begin by calling God our Father, which Jesus implies may be His favorite title.

Jesus called Him "Abba," which conveys intimacy, and told us to do the same. It's similar to when we address our earthly fathers as Daddy or Papa. It's warm and personal, familiar and comfortable. Rather than starting with a formal approach, we speak to God as His sons and daughters: "You have not received a spirit that makes you fearful slaves. Instead, you received God's

Spirit when he adopted you as his own children. Now we call him, 'Abba, Father'" (Romans 8:15 NLT).

God wants to be in an intimate relationship with you. And your relationship with Him begins with a right view of God. Nothing will determine your relationship with God more than your view of Him. Addressing Him as your Father still shows respect but accurately demonstrates your access and closeness.

When my kids were little, I loved nothing more than for them to jump in my lap, cuddle up, and tell me about their day. As they grew into adulthood, our communication wasn't as physically close, but the love, familiarity, and intimacy remained. They know they can come to me anytime—not just when they're struggling or needing something. I love it when they pop in and just say, "Hey, Dad, how are you? What are you working on? How's your day going?"

God loves for us to come to Him in this same way—as children who love Him and want to spend time with Him.

Hallowed Be Your Name: Start with Worship

After "Our Father in heaven," Jesus instructs us to take our relationship with our heavenly Father even further—"hallowed be Your name." *Hallow* isn't a word we use when we're talking and texting today. It means to revere, bless, and honor. Basically, we are to *worship* God's name.

When we pray, we need to know His name and use His name.

We find safety and security in hallowing His name: "GOD's name is a place of protection—good people can run there and be safe" (Proverbs 18:10 THE MESSAGE). His name is powerful and carries authority. When we trust in His name, we can access this same authority and power.

This authority reminds me of how I used to send one of my kids upstairs to tell their siblings to pick up their rooms. If they simply made this request without mentioning me, those rooms still wouldn't be picked up. But if they announced, "*Dad said* to tell you to pick up your rooms," they knew whose authority was being invoked and they'd spring into action. When we worship God's name, we show the same respect for His authority.

And to be completely accurate, we should worship not just one but *all* of God's many names. While there are many more, I usually include seven of His names when I pray: Righteousness, Sanctifier, Healer, Banner of Victory, Shepherd, Peace, and Provider. I might pray, "Father, You are my Righteousness, and through the gift of Your Son, You make me clean," or "Lord, You are the Healer over all afflictions, ailments, illnesses, and injuries—praise You!" I go through each of these seven and offer praise and worship related to what's going on in my life and how I need His presence in my life.

There are many other names and attributes of God for you to worship. Each name reflects part of His character and reveals new aspects of your relationship with Him. "Hallowed be Your name" is not intended to be an option mentioned in passing—it's foundational to knowing your Father completely. When you pray, worshiping God for who He is should always be part of your conversation with Him. He doesn't need to be reminded of who He is—but we do. Exploring the many amazing aspects of God's character compels us to worship because we can't help but appreciate His greatness. The Lord is more than worthy of our praise!

Your Kingdom Come: Pray the Father's Agenda First

Once we've addressed our Father and worshiped His names, Jesus told us to pray, "Your kingdom come. Your will be done on earth as it is in heaven." This means we pray our Father's agenda first. In any relationship, it's almost always a good idea to begin with "your" instead of "my," and certainly that's the case when we're talking to Almighty God, Creator of heaven and earth.

So often we jump right in by asking God for what we want before even considering what *He* wants. Have you ever considered how rude it is to ask all the time? When our immediate refrain is "gimme, gimme, gimme," we're seeing God only as a celestial Santa Claus. By acknowledging His kingdom and His will and praying that they would extend from heaven to earth, we're respecting that His ways are always better than ours.

Every strong relationship focuses on establishing connection before getting transactional.

When we pray His agenda over ours and put His priorities first, He enjoys having our hearts focused on Him. And when we do, the Bible tells us, "He will always give you all you need from day to day if you will make the Kingdom of God your primary concern" (Luke 12:31 TLB).

What is God's top priority and primary agenda? People. "For God so loved the world that He gave His only begotten Son . . ." (John 3:16 NKJV). Our Father wants our hearts to ache for the lost as much as His does.

Give Us This Day: Depend on Him for Everything

With our greetings, worship, and focus on God established, Jesus told us then to pray, "Give us this day our daily bread." Now that we've spent time with our attention solely on God, we can bring up our concerns, our needs, and our requests. We can make known our petitions and express our dependence on Him as the source of everything we have.

I suspect many people overlook praying, "Give us this day . . ." when things are going well and most of their needs are covered. When we're enjoying His blessings and experiencing times of smooth sailing, we may not have the motivation, urgency, or reliance on God for our needs.

But when we pray, "Give us," we're acknowledging that God has everything we need. The psalmist expressed this kind of dependence when he said, "I look up to the mountains—does my help come from there? My help comes from the LORD, who made heaven and earth!" (Psalm 121:1–2 NLT). What may sound like a rhetorical question here actually has a literal aspect to it. Looking up to the mountains does not refer to gazing toward heaven and God. In ancient Jerusalem, the government leaders' headquarters were on the hills, or mountains, above most of the city. So the psalmist was basically asking, "Does my help come from those in earthly power?"

It would be like you or me asking, "Does our help come from the Capitol? From the White House? From Washington, DC?" For us as well as the psalmist, the answer is the same. "No, my help comes only from God, maker of heaven and earth!"

Regardless of your needs, whether great or small, pray as if you have nothing except what God gives you for today. Depend on Him for everything all the time. Praise Him as your Source—everything you have and everything you need comes from Him.

As His beloved son or daughter, you can also ask your Father for what you want and need today. God is a giver with unlimited generosity toward His children. Just as we would never fail to give our children what they need, God never withholds His resources from us. Jesus reinforced this point later when He said:

> "Which of you, if your son asks for bread, will give him a stone? Or if he asks for a fish, will give him a snake? If you, then, though you are evil, know how to give good gifts to your children, how much more will your Father in heaven give good gifts to those who ask him!" (Matthew 7:9–11 NIV)

God wants to give His children good gifts. We simply need to acknowledge our dependence on God and then make our requests known to Him. He already knows what we need, but relying on Him for our daily bread keeps us humble, grateful, and secure in our faith.

Forgive Us Our Debts: Get Your Heart Right

The next aspect of prayer Jesus instructs us to include is confession: "Forgive us our debts, as we forgive our debtors." Notice the two parts of this focus on forgiveness. First, we confess our sins and shortcomings to God and ask Him to purify our hearts and attitudes. Then the emphasis shifts to how we reflect this forgiveness with other people. Simply put, we need to get our hearts right with God *and* with people. Forgiven people forgive people!

When we ask God's forgiveness here, we want Him to search us and reveal those dark places in our hearts that we can't or don't want to see. The goal here is to make sure we stay sensitive to sin, to anything that can come between us and God. This awareness keeps us mindful of the unfathomable gift of grace we have through the price Jesus paid for our sins on the cross. "If we confess our sins, he is faithful and just and will forgive us our sins and purify us from all unrighteousness" (1 John 1:9 NIV).

As we experience God's forgiveness, we also extend it to those around us. Jesus said that we should pray and ask God to forgive us as we forgive others. We experience the Lord's forgiveness to the degree we forgive those who have offended, hurt, or injured us. If we're harboring a grudge, bitterness, resentment, or revenge against someone, then we're blocking our ability to receive the free gift of God's grace.

When I pray on this aspect of forgiveness, I forgive not only those who have hurt me already but also those who will hurt me that day. I find it's easier to do in advance than after the fact so it keeps my heart focused on grace and an attitude of compassion. Anytime I'm about to drive on the highway, I pray in advance to forgive others because I know myself and other people too well!

Forgiveness keeps the lines of communication open between you and God as well as between you and other people.

Deliver Us: Spiritual Warfare

The next aspect of prayer Jesus instructed us to use often confuses some people: "And do not lead us into temptation, but deliver us from the evil one." Reading this, they will ask me, "Does God lead us into temptation? What's up with that?"

No, God does not lead us into temptation. He may allow us to face a trial or temptation, but He does not actively tempt us. Some scholars have argued that a better, more accurate translation of the original Greek might be "Do not allow us *to be led* into temptation." See the difference? We will face temptation presented by the Enemy today, so we need God's help to resist and stand strong in our faith. God does not lead us to sin—we get there just fine by ourselves. But He can fortify us and empower us to resist the traps the devil is waiting to spring on us.

Believe me, the Enemy is always plotting, scheming, and working to bring about our downfall. We're warned, "Be alert and of sober mind. Your enemy the devil prowls around like a roaring lion looking for someone to devour" (1 Peter 5:8 NIV). If you're not fighting the devil every day, then he's working harder than you!

If you're not fighting the devil every day, then he's working harder than you!

We call this "spiritual warfare," but don't be intimidated by this term. Some people freak out when they hear "spiritual warfare," while others may laugh and dismiss it. Remember, prayer is foremost communion with God, but it's also confrontation with the devil. "For our struggle is not against flesh and blood, but against the rulers, against the authorities, against the powers of this dark world and against the spiritual forces of evil in the heavenly realms" (Ephesians 6:12 NIV).

Confronting the Enemy means casting down every lie—everything not aligned with God's will—and replacing it with truth. It means binding the devil and his schemes against you and your family and those you love in the name of Jesus. It means standing strong in the protective authority of your heavenly Father.

When you pray, you take your stand against the Enemy.

Every day, you fight the good fight of faith.

Kingdom, Power, and Glory: A Catalyst for Your Faith

Finally, Jesus instructs us to conclude where we began by expressing faith in God's ability: "For Yours is the kingdom and the power and the glory forever." Keep in mind, God already knows His ability—when we pray this way, we're reminding ourselves of how amazing, limitless, and glorious He is in every way. I like to think of concluding my prayer time this way as a catalyst for releasing my faith.

I also love the way these phrases can lead us to other verses and passages of Scripture that reference these attributes and reasons to worship God. For example:

- **"Yours is the kingdom"—All rule belongs to You!** "Yours, LORD, is the greatness and the power and the glory and the majesty and the splendor, for everything in heaven and earth is yours. Yours, LORD, is the kingdom; you are exalted as head over all" (1 Chronicles 29:11 NIV).
- **"Yours is the power"—All mightiness flows from You!** "Ah, Sovereign LORD, you have made the heavens and the earth by your great power and outstretched arm. Nothing is too hard for you" (Jeremiah 32:17 NIV).
- **"Yours is the glory"—Your victory shall be complete!** "To him who sits on the throne and to the Lamb be praise and honor and glory and power, for ever and ever!" (Revelation 5:13 NIV).

God already knows
His ability—when we
pray this way, we're
reminding ourselves
of how amazing,
limitless, and glorious
He is in every way.

What a perfect way to conclude your time of communion with God! And remember, that's what prayer is all about—growing closer to your Father. You don't have to be formal and approach Him like a stern judge or unknowable entity—you can talk to Him like your Daddy who knows you and loves you.

You can develop your relationship by getting to know Him, focusing on His names and worshiping Him for all He is. You can put His agenda first and make His priority—loving people—your priority. You can receive His forgiveness to the extent you're willing to grant it to those who sin against you. In the fullness of His authority and power, you can confront the Enemy and disarm his ability to thwart your path. Finally, you can release your faith in God by acknowledging and celebrating His kingdom, His power, and His glory.

As Jesus told us, "This, then, is how you should pray" (Matthew 6:9 NIV). He instructed us with the perfect model of prayer that's both comprehensive and concise. Learning to pray the Lord's Prayer as a model of how to talk with God forever changed my view of prayer. As you learn to pray first, I hope it has the same effect on you!

seven

the prayer of Moses

———————

Who among the gods
is like you, LORD?
Who is like you—
majestic in holiness,
awesome in glory,
working wonders?

—Exodus 15:11 NIV

The Bible talks a lot about having regular conversation with God, but there are only a handful of actual prayers recorded in Scripture, excluding the many songs of worship and praise found in the Psalms. Nonetheless, we find many symbolic, historical elements that point to prayer models we can use today. Why would we do this? Because God's Word is clear that we're to pray continually and creatively: "Pray in the Spirit in *every situation*. Use *every kind* of prayer and request there is" (Ephesians 6:18 GW, emphasis added).

Most of us usually default to the one way we know to pray, often the method we learned growing up or when we first became a follower of Jesus. While we all need a foundational starting point, it's easy for our default prayer method to become so familiar and routine that we get stuck—all the more reason to seek out other models that can engage us at a deeper level.

As we explored in the last chapter, Jesus gave us an outline for communicating with God in the Lord's Prayer. When I learned that Jesus taught us elements of prayer and not a script to follow, it revolutionized my prayer life. And when my pastor taught me another model, called the Tabernacle Prayer, it immediately became my favorite way to pray. Even today, I follow this model, which I call the Prayer of Moses, more than any other. I'm delighted to share it with you, and I hope that you experience its benefits as much as I have.

Principle, Not Law

You may recall the story of Moses, the leader God chose to bring the Hebrew people out of slavery in Egypt. They were going to the promised land, which became the geographical nation of Israel. Once settled there, they were instructed to build a temple, which would be the permanent dwelling place of God among them. The Ten Commandments, which Moses received from God and delivered to the Israelites, represented God's presence and would also be stored in the temple.

The only problem, though, is that the people of Israel wandered in the desert for forty years before entering the promised land—which meant they needed a portable version of the temple to transport with them along the way. This portable version was called the tabernacle and comprised a rectangular tent with six pieces of furniture, built to God's specific instructions. "Have the people of Israel build me a holy sanctuary so I can live among them. You must build this Tabernacle and its furnishings exactly according to the pattern I will show you" (Exodus 25:8–9 NLT). Notice the purpose of the tabernacle—"So I can live among them." I love how God wants to be with us.

These instructions included a protocol for entering the presence of God. Moses would follow specific steps to communicate with the Lord—and not simply communicate with Him but enjoy intimate conversation: "Inside the Tent of Meeting, the LORD would speak to Moses face to face, as one speaks to a friend" (Exodus 33:11 NLT).

Can you imagine how incredible it must have been to directly experience the presence of the living God? You can experience this, too, and that's when prayer gets amazing. Your connection becomes so real that you know you're talking with God and He's talking to you. So can we still use this Old Testament pattern now that we live in the freedom of Christ as found in the New Testament?

Yes, but with a major difference—not as *law* but as *principle*. Jesus said, "Do not think that I have come to abolish the Law or the Prophets; I have not come to abolish them but to fulfill them" (Matthew 5:17 NIV). Jesus came to reveal the real meaning and purpose of the Law—connection with God—without that connection remaining contingent on our behavior. Christ permanently fulfilled the requirements of the Law and paid our debt for sin. For our purposes, those seven steps that Moses followed in the tabernacle are not mandatory requirements for entering God's presence but a model for drawing closer to Him.

With this goal in mind, let's tour the tabernacle and its six pieces of furniture to see how they can guide us closer to God.

The Outer Court: Begin with Thanksgiving and Praise

Approaching the tabernacle, Moses would have stepped into the outer court. Here, he would give God thanks, a tradition the psalmist later urged us to follow as well: "Enter his gates with thanksgiving and his courts with praise; give thanks to him and praise his name" (Psalm 100:4 NIV). Giving thanks is how you praise God, and it's a wonderful way to begin your prayer time.

It's easy to begin praying by telling God what you want and need. But before we ask Him for more, we need to stop and give thanks for what we have already received. Gratitude is one of the most powerful ways to keep our emotions balanced and healthy.

Gratitude is one of the most powerful ways to keep our emotions balanced and healthy. When we focus on all God has done for us and given us, we realize how blessed we are.

When we focus on all God has done for us and given us, we realize how blessed we are.

Whether I'm praying the Prayer of Moses through the tabernacle or not, I try to begin talking to God each day by first thanking Him—for a good night's sleep, for a new day, for my cup of coffee, for a healthy body, for my wife and children and grandchildren, for my Highlands family and the privilege of doing what God has called me to do. Because I'm prone to just go over the same list of blessings when I thank Him, I try to think of a fresh reason to thank Him every day, something I may have been overlooking or taking for granted.

No matter what your circumstances, your losses, or your disappointments, every human being has reasons to thank God. Giving thanks in the outer court adjusts the attitude of your heart and sets the tone for your next step in drawing closer to God—toward the brazen altar.

The Brazen Altar: Sinners Restored by the Cross

The brazen altar was where Moses offered a sacrifice to God in order to atone for his human sinfulness. According to God's law, blood had to be shed to pay for sins committed, which temporarily facilitated forgiveness and cleansing. So the brazen altar was usually covered in blood with animal carcasses smoldering. Moses would have to go right by this altar to get to God. Seeing the bloody remnants of all the sacrifices made likely called to mind his sins and mistakes.

Praise God we don't have to sacrifice animals anymore! Jesus' blood was the ultimate sacrifice. But the brazen altar reminds us that the only way we get to God is through the cross of Christ. We consider His sacrificial gift and experience gratitude for His willingness to do what we could never do. We're told, "When we were utterly helpless, Christ came at just the right time and died for us sinners" (Romans 5:6 NLT).

When I pray using this model, the brazen altar reminds me of the suffering Jesus endured on my behalf. Leading up to His death by crucifixion, Jesus received four major wounds: He was whipped, crowned with thorns, nailed to the cross in his hands and feet, and stabbed in His side by a spear. Anticipating these four wounds the Messiah would suffer, the prophet Isaiah reminds us what the cross did for us: "But he was pierced for our transgressions, he was crushed for our iniquities; the punishment that brought us peace was on him, and by his wounds we are healed" (Isaiah 53:5 NIV).

Notice the symbolic weight each wound carries. For our transgressions, the sinful actions and selfish disobedience to God, Jesus was pierced in His hands and feet. For our iniquities, the sinful nature we're born into, Jesus was crushed by the spear of a Roman guard. The distinction between transgressions and iniquities is important. Transgressions reflect what we've done and said and how we've behaved toward others. Iniquities refer to who we are, our identity apart from Christ, including all the lust, pride, deceit, and bitterness. Through His suffering and death on the cross, Jesus covers both our transgressions and our iniquities.

Punished by a crown of thorns intended to mock Him as

King of the Jews, Jesus enables us to have divine peace that passes understanding. When I consider the thorns crowning His head, I let go of all the fear, worry, anxiety, and stress in my mind. Jesus brings peace to our minds so I can let go of all the runaway thoughts and mind games I'm prone to sink into.

Finally, through the raw lash marks from being whipped, Jesus heals us. He heals our infirmities and diseases, our weaknesses and injuries, our relationships and our broken lives. Jesus heals the "dis-ease" in all areas of our lives—physically, spiritually, and emotionally.

Jesus heals the "dis-ease" in all areas of our lives— physically, spiritually, and emotionally.

I've shared how important music is to my prayer time. When I'm praying the Prayer of Moses, I'll often find a hymn or song for each stop within the tabernacle. At the brazen altar I often sing "Jesus Paid It All." I love the way this hymn so beautifully summarizes the eternal impact of my Savior's sacrifice: "Jesus paid it all, all to him I owe, sin had left a crimson stain, he washed it white as snow."

The Laver: Clean and Consecrated Hearts

The third step brings us to what's known as the laver, which was a place for washing oneself before proceeding any closer to the holiness of God. Basically, the laver of the tabernacle featured a large, shallow basin of water with mirrors on the bottom. As you washed yourself, you could see your condition and cleanse accordingly. Today when we pray, the laver reminds us to offer every part of our lives to God.

The laver may be my favorite part of the Prayer of Moses. It may sound goofy, but I start at the top of my head and offer every part of my body to God and pray to receive His cleansing touch. Offering my mind and all my thoughts, assumptions, and attitudes, I then pray for my eyes, asking the Lord to keep my vision focused on Him, on the needs of others, on what He wants me to do that day.

Then I'll focus on my ears and pray that I would listen to God's voice and not the temptations of the Enemy. Next, my mouth and tongue are offered for cleansing so that the words I say may be pleasing to God and not harmful toward others. From there, I move down to my hands and feet. I'll pray that my hands may be of service and touch others with God's love. I'll ask God to set my feet on course with where He wants me to go.

Throughout this process, I'm mindful that Jesus forgave us once and for all—His work is finished and my salvation is secured. But I'm also aware of wanting God to change me, cleanse me, renew me so that I might be more like Jesus. I'm reminded of what Paul urged believers in Rome: "Therefore, I urge you, brothers and sisters, in view of God's mercy, to offer your bodies as a living sacrifice, holy and pleasing to God—this is your true and proper worship" (Romans 12:1 NIV).

You probably won't be surprised to learn that my favorite song to sing at the laver is "Take My Life and Let It Be." Like my prayer of cleansing and consecration, this hymn voices my desire for God to work in all areas of my life and in all parts of my mind, heart, body, and soul.

The Candlestick: A Life Open to the Spirit

After the laver, the fourth step in Moses' prayer through the tabernacle brings us to the candlestick. Here, he would step into a smaller tent within the larger one of the entire structure. Inside the small tent, a candlestick with eight candles would be burning. This Jewish menorah symbolized the fire of God's presence, the refining power of His Spirit, and the anointing of His people with gifts and abilities. Today, the candlestick reminds us to invite the work of the Holy Spirit into our lives.

All throughout Scripture, fire represents the Spirit of God. At Pentecost when the early followers of Jesus received the gift of the Holy Spirit, it descended on each of them like a tongue of fire (Acts 2:3). The fire brings life, warmth, comfort, and illumination. God is alive in us, working and moving. The Holy Spirit enables us to say no to wrong things, guides us to do the right things, and empowers us with gifts to help other people.

Our role isn't a passive one, however, but a cooperative one with God's Spirit. Not only do we invite and accept Him into our lives, but through our prayers we experience the Spirit to maximum capacity in our lives. In the Bible we're encouraged to actively participate with all the Spirit wants to do in our lives: "This is why I remind you to fan into flames the spiritual gift God gave you when I laid my hands on you. For God has not given us a spirit of fear and timidity, but of power, love, and self-discipline" (2 Timothy 1:6–7 NLT). Notice that we have to fan the flame, to stir it up.

This element of the Moses Prayer reminds me to spend time before God asking Him to anoint me and use me for His purposes. I ask for spiritual gifts and seek to use the ones I've already received for the greatest eternal impact. Every living person has gifts, abilities, and a calling from God to use those talents for His kingdom. We have all we need through the power of Christ in us.

The Table of Showbread: Nourished by God's Promises

Speaking of all we need, after the candlestick comes the table of showbread. Stepping out of the small, candle-illuminated tent, Moses would step toward a table with twelve loaves of freshly baked bread. The aroma must have been amazing! Just think about places, like a bakery or kitchen, where the delicious scent of warm bread envelops you as soon as you walk in. Even imagining the taste of a hot-from-the-oven slice of bread makes me want to grab a slab of butter right now!

The table of showbread reminds us to feed on the promises in God's Word. As Jesus quoted from Scripture in response to the devil's temptation after Christ had been fasting for forty days in the desert, "It is written: 'Man shall not live on bread alone, but on every word that comes from the mouth of God'" (Matthew 4:4 NIV). Put another way, God's Word is our daily bread. Just as we need food to provide nourishment for our bodies, we need God's Word to nourish our spirits.

I always include scripture in my prayer time, so the table of showbread compels me to find a promise in God's Word and feed on it. The Lord speaks through His Word and strengthens us. We receive nourishment and power from the truth of His Word. "For the word of God is alive and active. Sharper than any double-edged sword, it penetrates even to dividing soul and spirit, joints and marrow; it judges the thoughts and attitudes of the heart" (Hebrews 4:12 NIV).

The Bible is more than instructive and inspirational, however. When we devour the Word, we also equip ourselves with offensive weaponry against our Enemy. We're instructed to "put on the full armor of God, so that you can take your stand against the devil's schemes" (Ephesians 6:11 NIV). Recall how Jesus wielded Scripture in each of His replies to the devil's three temptations after His time of prayer and fasting in the desert.

The Altar of Incense: Reverence and Adoration

Our next to the last stop as we walk with Moses through the tabernacle is at the altar of incense. Just before you parted the last curtain and entered the place where God dwelled, you likely smelled the sweet aroma emanating from a small altar. Using coals from the brazen altar, this smaller altar wafted the rich, aromatic smoke of incense to God as a sign of worship.

For twenty-four hours a day, incense burned as a tribute to Almighty God.

This stop reminds us to spend time worshiping God, offering our sweet-smelling prayers of joyful proclamation about our Father, Creator, and Giver of Life. You'll recall we began our prayer journey in the outer court, where we praised God by thanking Him for all He's done. Worship, like that offered at the altar of incense, thanks God simply for who He is. He is worthy of our worship just because He is Holy God, the Great I Am.

Worship facilitates intimacy with the Father. You just sing and love Him with all your heart. You celebrate God for lavishly loving you as His child. Along with the psalmist, you can sing, "Come, let us bow down in worship, let us kneel before the LORD our Maker; for he is our God and we are the people of his pasture, the flock under his care" (Psalm 95:6–7 NIV).

Worship facilitates intimacy with the Father. You just sing and love Him with all your heart. You celebrate God for lavishly loving you as His child.

The word *worship* comes from the root word *worth*. When we worship the Lord, we sing about His worth, not our own or anyone else's. Worth is reflected by the names someone has, and the same is true of God. His worth is revealed in His names. "The name of the LORD is a fortified tower; the righteous run to it and are safe" (Proverbs 18:10 NIV).

As discussed in the previous chapter, I absolutely love worshiping God by focusing on His various names. When I get to this point in the Prayer of Moses, I often think of the names Holy, Righteous, Peace, Counselor, Friend, Shepherd, Healer, Provider, Defender, and Always There. Praying these names allows me to appreciate God more fully and comprehensively and adore Him for all these facets. Praying this way reminds me of a text I received from my son David a few years ago. He was pastoring in California, and while we missed each other and talked frequently, he rarely sent me texts. But one day out of the blue, David texted: "I love you, Dad. I think you're a GREAT man!"

His words penetrated my heart deeply. I felt seen and appreciated and valued and honored and loved all at once, which is probably similar to how God feels when we worship Him.

The Mercy Seat: Intercession

Finally, after going through the tabernacle, Moses would reach the ark of the covenant, the special piece of furniture where God dwelled among His people, in the form of either a cloud or a fire. Similar to a small bench or backless chair, known as the mercy seat, the ark had two golden angels both covering their eyes, one guarding each side. If you've seen *Raiders of the Lost Ark*, you probably recall how the ark was depicted—and more dramatically, the impact it had on those who looked upon it!

Before the mercy seat of God, the Jewish priests would stand and intercede for others, pleading their case much like a lawyer before a judge in court. The priest was there to stand in the gap for others, to beseech God to meet their needs and answer their requests. This is the same role we step into at this last station: to intercede for others. We cry out to God and lift up the needs of those we know and love.

This is also where we intercede for those with authority over us. The Bible tells us, "I urge, then, first of all, that petitions, prayers, intercession and thanksgiving be made for all people—for kings and all those in authority, that we may live peaceful and quiet lives in all godliness and holiness" (1 Timothy 2:1–2 NIV). Our prayer intercession should include all those in any kind of authority or leadership, whether spiritual, civil, work-related, or parental. We include the leaders of our nation, state, city, community, and church.

This is when I pray for God to work locally and personally as well as globally and comprehensively. I often pray for freedom from bondage, blessing over trouble, wisdom for the future, victory over the Enemy, and healing for all dis-eases in my life and in the lives of those I lift up. Closing out my prayer time with these intercessions, following the other six steps in the Prayer of Moses, leaves me feeling whole, complete, and intimately connected to God.

While using the Moses Prayer may sound time-consuming or intricate, it's really much easier to experience than I can describe. This prayer is my favorite because it focuses us on the process for entering the presence of God. I feel like I'm walking through this protocol, taking steps in a sacred place, moving closer and closer to the Lord waiting on the mercy seat.

Yes, we have direct access to our heavenly Father now. When Jesus died on the cross, "the curtain of the temple was torn in two from top to bottom" (Matthew 27:51 NIV)—signifying that the ultimate sacrifice had been made so that we could now experience personal relationship with God. The Prayer of Moses reminds us to savor the various aspects, historical and spiritual, of our faith as we come into God's presence.

eight

the prayer of Jabez

Aim at Heaven and you will get Earth "thrown
in": aim at Earth and you will get neither.

—C. S. Lewis

If the Prayer of Moses is my favorite way to pray, then the
Prayer of Jabez is my favorite prayer to pray. I love how concise and
yet comprehensive this little prayer is. I can pray it in two minutes
or linger over its four components for a half hour. The Prayer of
Jabez is found in the Old Testament book of 1 Chronicles, which
begins with nine chapters of genealogies. It's kind of funny to me
that in the middle of six hundred names, this one man is singled
out—and mentioned nowhere else in Scripture. Amid the dozens

of "and their descendants were" and "sons of," there's a pause for a brief, self-contained short story with a prayer showcased.

Descended from the tribe of Judah, Jabez is introduced to us with two almost contradictory pieces of information: "Jabez was more honorable than his brothers. His mother had named him Jabez, saying, 'I gave birth to him in pain'" (1 Chronicles 4:9 NIV). Before the reason for his name is revealed, Jabez is described as more honorable than his brothers, as if to overshadow his name's meaning. And his mother had named him Jabez because of the intense pain she experienced upon his delivery or perhaps because of challenging circumstances surrounding his birth.

Whether her pain was physical or emotional, or both, we're not told, but the fact that she chose this name, which sounds similar to the Hebrew word for "pain," speaks volumes. Clearly, it's not a good name to be given as you start life. Like the old Johnny Cash song about a "boy named Sue," Jabez likely drew a lot of unwanted attention because of his peculiar, unexpected name. Can't you imagine how the other kids must have picked on him! "Don't be such a Jabez in the neck!"

In ancient times, your name often defined you, possibly in a prophetic way as you became what you had been labeled at birth. This tendency endures even now. Perhaps the role you played in childhood—the troublemaker, the clown, the bully, the outsider—has followed you into adulthood.

But clearly Jabez wasn't willing to settle for a life of pain—and neither should you.

Pray for Blessing

Rather than settle for the default label he had been given at birth, Jabez prayed and received God's promise. Following his model, the Prayer of Jabez shows us how to overcome our own pain and suffering as well. Instead of ruminating on our anguish, we can fix our eyes on what God has for us beyond it.

I'm convinced this is the reason why God answered this man's prayer: Jabez was focused on God's good intentions for his life instead of being preoccupied with the past and the pain of his namesake. "Jabez cried out to the God of Israel, 'Oh, that you would *bless me* and *enlarge* my territory! Let your *hand* be with me, and *keep me* from harm so that I will be free from pain.' And *God granted his request*" (1 Chronicles 4:10 NIV, emphasis added). Notice that Jabez asked four requests of God: for blessing, influence, presence, and protection. Let's consider each of these and how they can inform our prayers today.

First, Jabez prayed for God's favor—"Oh, that you would bless me . . ." (v. 10 NIV). The original Hebrew language for "bless me" here derives from *barak*, meaning to kneel, to stoop down. Jabez asked the Lord to bend down and put His hand on him, to reach from heaven and touch his life on earth. It's the same image we find in the Psalms: "You protect me with your saving shield. You support me with your right hand. You have *stooped to make me great*" (18:35 NCV, emphasis added).

There's a lot of misunderstanding about the concept of blessings, both inside and outside the church. Some people think it's all about health and wealth, name it and claim it, blab it and grab it. But that's not what Jabez was asking for. He asked God to impart His supernatural favor and then some. This kind of blessing is on steroids with added exclamation marks! When God stoops down to make us great, our lives overflow with abundance in every area.

In fact, God wants to bless us—it's His nature as a Father who lavishly loves His children to pour out His blessings on us. But the reason He blesses us is not so we can be rich and have a lot of stuff and live a life of comfort and leisure. God's Word tells us, "I will bless you . . . and you will be a blessing to others" (Genesis 12:2 NLT). We are blessed to be a blessing!

If you're not blessed, then your ability to bless others remains limited.

Many people don't pray this way because they're too focused on their own pain instead of the needs of others. Some ask for blessing but really just want to compensate for past losses or deprivations. They want to feel good about themselves based on their bank accounts or material possessions instead of basing their identity in Jesus Christ. There's nothing wrong with money and possessions, and God often blesses us with them—but not so we can stockpile them for security. The Lord entrusts us to be His stewards and use what we have so that others may know Him and experience the love of Jesus.

When I pray for God's blessings, I ask Him, "Lord, give me more than I need so that I can be a blessing to the world around me." I'm not telling you this to blow my own horn. I'm simply sharing how I view this prayer request and exercise it accordingly. Pray for blessing so that you can bless others around you.

Pray for Influence

This leads us to Jabez's second request: "... enlarge my territory ..." (1 Chronicles 4:10 NIV). This doesn't mean Jabez only wanted more acreage—he was asking God for a greater sphere of influence. Landowners determined how people living on their land would be treated. By asking God to enlarge his territory, Jabez wanted to be able to show more people the kindness and goodness of the God he served.

The same is true today. Once you have blessing, God wants to use you to make a difference. As a conduit of His power and resources, you have the ability to advance God's kingdom and impact lives for eternity. People who pray the prayer of influence are the happiest people I know because they have something bigger to live for than eliminating their personal pain. Rather than focus on what they have or don't have in their lives, they concentrate on fulfilling the purpose God has for them to carry out.

This explains why the apostle Paul prayed for believers in the early church to see beyond their circumstances: "I pray that the eyes of your heart may be enlightened in order that you may know the hope to which he has called you, the riches of his glorious inheritance in his holy people" (Ephesians 1:18 NIV). Seeing with the eyes of our hearts enlarges our vision far beyond our own welfare, comfort, and benefit. Praying this way, we see others with the compassion of Christ.

Praying for influence is one of the most important prayers you can pray. When you're willing to pray, "Lord, show me my calling, show me the legacy You want me to leave," you discover the joy of significance and contentment. Knowing and living out your purpose gives your life meaning.

This isn't simply my opinion. God's Word tells us, "Ask me, and I will make the nations your inheritance, the ends of the earth your possession" (Psalm 2:8 NIV). God wants us to invest in the only thing that lasts forever—people. Houses and cars and boats don't last. Clothes and jewelry and gadgets won't be here. Nothing lasts for eternity except human beings created in the image of their Creator, Almighty God.

I encourage you to dream while you pray. Write down images and visions you receive in pursuit of the dreams God gives you. Do you know how you can tell if those dreams are from God? If they're impossible for you to accomplish without Him! If the size of your dream isn't intimidating to you, then there's a good chance it isn't what God has in mind for you.

When you ask God to enlarge your territories, you're requesting a life of excitement, adventure, and fulfillment in pursuit of what matters most. When God answers your prayer and uses you to influence others, your pain no longer preoccupies your life. Suddenly, your vision allows you to see things closer to the way God sees them. You realize just how powerful God really is and how loving and tender His heart is for His children.

I remember experiencing this sense of expansion when I stood in Red Square in Moscow along with a group of twenty college students. Standing there and praying for the people of what was then known as the USSR to know God and for the government to allow churches and Bibles and missionaries—that was the fulfillment of a prayer I'd made to God many years prior. As a young man discovering my passion for God, I had asked God for something that seemed audacious and nearly impossible. With the Cold War still in its decades-long deep freeze, I had prayed for God to allow me to go to Red Square and proclaim the gospel of Jesus to the Russian people. Then years later, there I stood!

You were created to be an influencer—and I don't mean the kind on social media. You may not know your purpose yet or the extent of it, but God does. He wants to show you and empower you to do what seems impossible to you now. I've never stopped praying for the Lord to enlarge my influence: "God, show me Your purpose for my life so I can live a life bigger than my own." I dare you to pray your own version of this request and see what happens!

Pray for Presence

Once you are blessed and God is giving you influence, then you'll need to rely on Him more than ever. That's why we follow the example of Jabez and pray, "Let your hand be with me . . ." (1 Chronicles 4:10 NIV). In the Scriptures this term, "the hand of the Lord," conveys God's presence and power. For example, we're told, "The Lord's hand was with them, and a great number of people believed and turned to the Lord" (Acts 11:21 NIV).

With blessing and opportunity will come the need for God's presence 24–7. Because the more resources and responsibilities you're given, the more humbled you will become as you realize

You may not know
your purpose yet
or the extent of
it, but God does.
He wants to show
you and empower
you to do what
seems impossible
to you now.

you're unable to accomplish the goals set before you by yourself. Even when you've walked with God, relied on His power, and watched Him do incredible, humanly impossible things, you will still feel helpless unless you continue experiencing His presence. As you mature in your faith, you learn to walk in His presence, moment by moment and day by day.

I know it feels better to us if we believe we're qualified and competent, educated and trained for the purpose and opportunities colliding before us. But it doesn't take long to realize that no matter how many credentials or how much experience we have, it's ultimately never enough. Because only God can accomplish the impossible—and He prefers to reveal His power and greatness through those who serve Him.

In fact, God likes to use foolish things—situations and events, people and relationships that simply don't make sense—to accomplish what needs doing. God has called me and everyone at Church of the Highlands to do more than we're qualified to do. This is why we continue to rely on Him through prayer. Our church was started with 21 Days of Prayer because we were so in over our heads. More than two decades later, we are sustained by continuing to pray—because we remain desperate for God's presence. I want His presence in the way that Moses asked God to give it:

> Then Moses said to him, "If your Presence does not go with us, do not send us up from here. How will anyone know that you are pleased with me and with your people unless you go with us? What else will distinguish me and your people from all

the other people on the face of the earth?" And the LORD said to Moses, "I will do the very thing you have asked." (Exodus 33:15–17 NIV)

Basically, we can do nothing on our own—but we can do all things through Christ who strengthens us (Philippians 4:13). We pray, "Lord, be with us because what You've called us to do is too big for us to do apart from You."

Pray for Protection

If you've received God's blessing, influence, and presence, then I have some bad news for you: all of hell will try to stop you. That's why we pray like Jabez and ask God, ". . . keep me from harm" (1 Chronicles 4:10 NIV). You may be under attack right now, even as you're reading the words on this page. You may assume it's circumstantial, but actually the enemy of your soul is trying to keep you distracted from relying on God and living out your purpose. It is not accidental. It is spiritual.

The last thing the devil wants is for you to be experiencing the fullness of all God has for you—His blessings, His influence, and His presence in your life. And the Enemy pulls out all the stops with as much force as he can muster: "The devil prowls around like a roaring lion looking for someone to devour" (1 Peter 5:8 NIV).

Remember, Jesus taught us to pray, "And lead us not into temptation, but deliver us from the evil one" (Matthew 6:13 NIV). We ask God not only for victory in the midst of attacks and temptations but also for protection from the Enemy's assaults before they occur. No matter what I'm praying, I like to include this request: "Lord, strengthen me and protect me from every attack of the Enemy."

The devil wants you to focus on your pain—to focus on escaping it, comforting yourself from it, or wallowing in it as a victim. But when you focus on what God wants, then you can trust that your pain will no longer be the center of your life. Paul expressed it well: "Who shall separate us from the love of Christ? Shall trouble or hardship or persecution or famine or nakedness or danger or sword? . . . No, in all these things we are more than conquerors through him who loved us" (Romans 8:35, 37 NIV).

Simply put, you can focus on getting God focused on what you want.

Or you can focus on what God wants.

And in the process of focusing on what God wants—you get what you want.

God granted the four requests Jabez made—for blessing, influence, presence, and protection—and He will do the same for you.

Prayer isn't about God moving toward you. *Prayer is about you moving toward God.*

Remember, prayer isn't about God moving toward you.

Prayer is about you moving toward God.

nine

the prayer of the sheep

———————

Prayer is not overcoming God's reluctance,
but laying hold of His willingness.

—Martin Luther

We all have names that reflect our roles, experiences, characters, and unique personalities. Mine include Chris and Pastor Chris and PC (from people at church and our staff), Honey (from my wife), Dad (from my kids), and now Papa (from my grandkids). A few close friends call me Hodge or Preacher, and if someone calls me Mr. Hodges, they probably don't know me very well.

The names we use to address God are even more significant.

So far in this section I've shared with you my favorite way to pray (the Prayer of Moses) as well as my favorite prayer (the Prayer of Jabez). Now I want to share with you a way to pray that pleases God while helping us know more of who He is and what He's like. I love praying this way and try to include at least some of the descriptive names of God every time I pray.

Why is it so important to pray the names of God? Because praying this way focuses our attention on His qualities, His abilities, and His nature. If we're not careful, it's far too easy to make our prayers all about us.

If we're not careful, it's far too easy to make our prayers all about us.

We've probably all endured conversations that were more like monologues as a friend, neighbor, or coworker talked our ears off. They shared anything and everything about themselves without allowing us to get a word in edgewise, as my daddy used to say. None of us want to come across that way when talking to other people, so we shouldn't slip into this habit by default when talking to God.

Instead of focusing on ourselves, praying the names of God makes it all about Him. Then when we make our requests and petitions known, we're communicating confidence in who He is and not merely what He does for us. Basically, we're telling God, "I'm expecting You to answer this prayer *because of who You are.*" We encounter Him on His own terms, not ours. We make it clear that we want to know all aspects of God and the fullness of His character.

Another compelling reason to pray the names of God is

simply because Jesus included this approach when teaching His followers how to pray: "Our Father in heaven, *hallowed* be your *name*" (Matthew 6:9 NIV, emphasis added). This reinforces the third commandment that God included with the ten given to Moses after God delivered the people of Israel from Egypt: "You shall not take the name of the LORD your God in vain, for the LORD will not hold him guiltless who takes His name in vain" (Exodus 20:7 NKJV). Taking the Lord's name in vain includes more than just swearing (or cussing, as we say in my neck of the woods). Anytime we misuse God's name, we disrespect who He is. Using God's name carelessly dilutes the reverence we should have for it.

Finally, we should pray the names of God in order to exercise God's power and authority over all situations. Paul tells us that God exalted Jesus to the highest place "and gave him the name that is above every name, that at the name of Jesus every knee should bow . . . and every tongue acknowledge that Jesus Christ is Lord, to the glory of God the Father" (Philippians 2:9–11 NIV). James adds that "even the demons believe—and tremble" (2:19 NKJV). When we pray the names of God, we're connecting to the Highest Authority.

We Are His Sheep

As we explored in chapter 5, praying to all three persons of God—Father, Son, and Holy Spirit—is a vital part of relating to God in His fullness. Similarly, praying additional names of God directs our attention to His many qualities, abilities, and attributes.

Throughout the Bible we find eight primary names by which God has been known to His people. While there are numerous ways to pray God's names based on examples in Scripture, one of my favorites reveals these eight different names and qualities of God—all in one concise, poetic passage.

This passage comes from one of the most beloved and well-known psalms in the Bible—Psalm 23. Like me, you may have memorized it when you were growing up. This psalm is all about Jesus as the Good Shepherd and how He takes care of us, His sheep:

> The LORD is my shepherd;
> I shall not want.
> He makes me to lie down in green pastures;
> He leads me beside the still waters.
> He restores my soul;
> He leads me in the paths of righteousness
> For His name's sake.
>
> Yea, though I walk through the valley of the
>   shadow of death,
> I will fear no evil;
> For You are with me;
> Your rod and Your staff, they comfort me.
>
> You prepare a table before me in the presence of my
>   enemies;
> You anoint my head with oil;

My cup runs over.

Surely goodness and mercy shall follow me

All the days of my life;

And I will dwell in the house of the LORD

Forever. (Psalm 23:1–6 NKJV)

Because this psalm is so familiar, I suspect you can identify some of the names and qualities of God embedded here but probably not all eight of them. So let's unpack these one by one and discover how this passage serves as the ideal template for what I like to call the Prayer of the Sheep.

You Are My Shepherd

First thing here, we're assured, "The LORD is my *shepherd*..." (23:1, emphasis added), which makes our prayers incredibly personal. We can trust that God leads, guards, nourishes, and protects us just as a shepherd would for his sheep.

In fact, this is the first name of God to celebrate in worship in this prayer: "You, Lord, are my Shepherd and I follow You!" This name is not simply metaphoric—it is *Jehovah-Raah*, the Hebrew covenant name for God. This literally means "pastor," which is another word for shepherd, one who leads and feeds his flock. Jesus told us, "I am the good shepherd; I know my sheep and my sheep know me" (John 10:14 NIV).

When you pray, "The Lord is my shepherd," you're placing yourself under His care by acknowledging and worshiping Him.

Jesus wants to be in a relationship with you by pastoring you as His follower. As your shepherd, He speaks and you listen, He guides and you follow, He corrects and you obey, He encourages and you rest in His love.

Allow me to make a sidenote here and remind you that everyone needs a pastor in their lives. Pastors embody the Shepherd-Spirit of Christ and provide instruction, wisdom, guidance, and encouragement as you grow in your faith. They nourish you with the Word of God and help you stay focused on prioritizing your relationship with God. They correct you when you go astray and serve as a conduit of God's mercy, grace, and forgiveness.

Everyone needs a pastor—even pastors! Yes, Jesus is our Chief Pastor and the ultimate Good Shepherd, but we all need someone who embodies this name and its qualities in our lives. I thank God for my pastor and the amazing help he has provided to guide me during difficult times. If you don't have a pastor at present, I urge you to make finding a church home and personal pastor a priority. You need the covering and community found there.

You Are My Provider

You also need your Good Shepherd to provide for you, which brings us to the second name and quality of God in Psalm 23, our Provider: "The LORD is my shepherd; *I shall not want*" (v. 1 NKJV, emphasis added). The Hebrew name is *Jehovah-Jireh,* which means "I will not lack." Praying this name asserts your trust and confidence in God to provide for all your needs.

Praying this name may sound easy enough—until you stop and realize how consistently we try to control circumstances and relationships ourselves. The tendency is to take care of yourself and defend against relying on anyone else. So many factors in our culture and global society today encourage us to be self-reliant, independent, and self-sufficient. Strength is equated with needing no one, while vulnerability is viewed as weakness.

Perhaps the primary way we're told to provide for ourselves is by making a lot of money. Many people put their trust in wealth and accumulating possessions. Rich people tend to live with a false sense of security, assuming that if they have enough money, they're secure. Financial security, however, is an illusion. If you ask most people what it would take for them to feel financially secure, they usually answer, "More than I have right now." Security based on dollar amounts is a trick of the Enemy to entice you to trust yourself instead of God. When you're relying on money, enough is never enough.

Which explains why those living in poverty, statistically, are on average more generous. They already know that their money can never give them hope and security. As followers of Jesus entrusting all areas of our lives to Him, we know that He is our only source of stability and protection. When we pray, "I shall not want," we declare that we are putting our trust not in riches but in Him who richly provides.

After all, why put your hope in the provision when you can put your hope in the Provider? God's Word promises, "And my God will meet all your needs according to the riches of his glory in Christ Jesus" (Philippians 4:19 NIV). Notice that it doesn't say *some* of your needs or a *few* of your needs but *all* of your needs. This certainty reminds us to exercise our trust not only in prayer but in giving tithes and offerings. By honoring God with the first of our abundance, we know we can rest in His provision. Praying to God as our Provider, we are able to let go of our concerns about our needs. Surrendering our needs to Him is a form of worship.

We can be generous because we trust the Source of all resources.

You Are My Peace

Next, we come to the third name and quality of God in our prayer model: God is our Peace. The psalmist described this beautifully with pastoral imagery: "He makes me to *lie down* in green pastures; He leads me beside the *still waters*" (Psalm 23:2 NKJV, emphasis added). This prayer seems more relevant than ever. God often has to "make us lie down" because we are so busy and refuse to slow down until we're forced to do so.

And what's the result of being made to lie down in green pastures and to follow our Shepherd beside the still waters? "He restores my soul" (Psalm 23:3 NKJV). When we pray to our God of Peace, we are addressing *Jehovah-Shalom*. The Hebrew word *shalom* means not only peace but also wholeness, completeness, and wellness. When we pray, "Lord, You are my Peace," we both celebrate and remind ourselves of our need to slow down and rest.

Today, most of us need more time in the green pastures beside still waters. The levels of stress, anxiety, and depression among people around the world continue to rise to unprecedented levels. Too many people I know carry around a constant burden of worries, stressors, and anxiety-inducing triggers. Most of them emerge from four main categories of stressors: work, money, family, and health.

However, if we know and trust the Lord, we do not have to live this way. Our God doesn't have peace that He dispenses when we need it—He is Peace! When we rest in Him, we experience the peace that passes human understanding, a supernatural sense of security and safety. Jesus told us, "Peace I leave with you; my peace I give you. I do not give to you as the world gives. Do not let your hearts be troubled and do not be afraid" (John 14:27 NIV).

We must practice slowing down and focusing on our priorities rather than allowing every urgent demand to rob us of time, energy, and peace. In Ecclesiastes we're told, "Better one handful with tranquility than two handfuls with toil and chasing after the wind" (4:6 NIV). In a world where we're constantly told to do more, have more, and go for more, we must remember that less—with God—is always better.

You Are My Healer

In addition to having our peace restored, God is also our Healer, or *Jehovah-Rapha*.

This Hebrew name means to restore by returning to the previous point of departure. God is the only One who can restore our health, minds, hearts, families, finances, and relationships

Our God doesn't have peace that He dispenses when we need it—He is Peace! When we rest in Him, we experience the peace that passes human understanding, a supernatural sense of security and safety.

back to the health and wholeness that He intended. This includes physical healing and healing in any other area of our lives.

In the New Testament, Peter explained this kind of healing and tied it directly to Jesus as our Shepherd: "He personally carried our sins in his body on the cross so that we can be dead to sin and live for what is right. By his wounds you are healed. Once you were like sheep who wandered away. But now you have turned to your Shepherd, the Guardian of your souls" (1 Peter 2:24–25 NLT). Our Good Shepherd provides restoration and healing for what's broken in us.

I'm a firm believer that this process takes place as described in God's Word—through God's presence in other people. We need to put down our defenses and allow others to know us and see us. The Bible tells us to confess our sins to God as a reminder to rely on His grace alone. We're also told, "Therefore confess your sins to each other and pray for each other so that you may be healed. The prayer of a righteous person is powerful and effective" (James 5:16 NIV).

At our church we know this usually takes place in the context of our small groups. Church of the Highlands has several thousand small groups going at any one time so everyone can find a tribe of like-minded believers who share their interests and areas they want to focus on: marriage, parenting, finances, overcoming depression, health and fitness, grief, recovery, hobbies, and seasons of life. This is where lives are changed and people experience healing from their brokenness. Small groups are a place to grow where iron sharpens iron.

God often chooses to heal us through His people.

You Are My Righteousness

God is not only our Shepherd, Provider, Peace, and Healer—He is also our Righteousness: "He leads me in the paths of righteousness for His name's sake" (Psalm 23:3 NKJV). The Hebrew tells us God is *Jehovah-Tsidkenu*, meaning He is not only our Righteousness but He makes us righteous as well. Through the blood of Jesus, we receive what we could not do for ourselves.

Notice in Psalm 23 that righteousness has a path. Our Shepherd always leads us in the right direction. Why? Because of who He is—"For His name's sake." As we follow the Lord on the path of righteousness, we become more and more like Christ. We're told, "For the LORD watches over the way of the righteous, but the way of the wicked leads to destruction" (Psalm 1:6 NIV).

Are you following God's path for your life? The one guided by His righteousness, for His name's sake? When we pray to God as our Righteousness, we submit our plans in order to follow His plans. We pray for His will to be done and not our own. We surrender our own agendas and let go of doing things our own way.

God is a holy God and His name is holy. He wants to lead us away from a compromised lifestyle. When we follow Him, God will deal with our character, our flesh, our choices, and our anger. Down the path of righteousness, we lose our bitterness, our sinful weakness, and our tendency to compromise and justify ourselves. "As obedient children, do not conform to the evil desires you had when you lived in ignorance. But just as he who called you is holy, so be holy in all you do" (1 Peter 1:14–15 NIV).

So many people say that they want God's will in their lives but don't follow the path of His righteousness. They tend to forget that He aligns before He assigns. God wants us in step with His Holy Spirit before He reveals His next assignment for us. If we stray off His path, we lose sight of living out our divine purpose.

You Are My Constant Companion

We are never alone as we walk by faith because God is our Constant Companion. Once again, the psalmist described it perfectly: "Yea, though I walk through the valley of the shadow of death, I will fear no evil; for You are with me; Your rod and Your staff, they comfort me" (Psalm 23:4 NKJV). This is God as *Jehovah-Shammah*, "The Lord Is There."

All of us go through times of isolation and darkness, but we are never alone. "God has said, 'Never will I leave you; never will I forsake you.' So we say with confidence, 'The Lord is my helper; I will not be afraid. What can mere mortals do to me?'" (Hebrews 13:5–6 NIV).

What a comfort to know that no matter what we're facing, we don't have to face it alone. God is there in the emergency room, in the courtroom, in the funeral home, in the boardroom, in the grocery store, in the classroom, in the midst of wherever we are. Why? Because it's who He is! The Lord Is There.

You might assume that the Shepherd's rod and staff were used for punishment. I've even heard some preachers mistakenly say that God uses these to strike us when we stray. But this is

God wants us in step
with His Holy Spirit
before He reveals
His next assignment
for us. If we stray
off His path, we lose
sight of living out
our divine purpose.

not accurate. A shepherd would use his rod and staff to protect his sheep by fighting back their enemies and predators, such as a wolf. God is there for us so we don't have to worry about being attacked without divine defense.

My wife, Tammy, and I were robbed shortly after we were married. One night while we were upstairs asleep, robbers cleaned out almost everything we owned on the first floor—appliances, camera, stereo, Tammy's purse, wall décor, and a nice clock. They left our furniture but both our cars had also been broken into and stripped of anything valuable. I'll never forget going downstairs that morning and seeing the front door swinging wide open in our living room. In addition to losing what little we had, we no longer felt safe and secure in our home.

We felt reassured, however, when the law enforcement deputy came to file our report and look for evidence. He could tell how shook up we were and told us, "I'm on duty tonight, and I'll be parked right over there where I can see your front door. If I have to leave, I'll send my replacement to stand guard. You can rest easy tonight." I'll forever be grateful for his kindness in helping us reclaim our sense of being safe in our own home.

This is the kind of reassurance we can enjoy all the time. Yes, thieves broke in and took our stuff, but it wasn't worth that much anyway. We were both unharmed and experienced kindness from those committed to serving and protecting us. God was still with us even in the midst of something scary and unexpected. God is the God of Being There—always.

You Are My Defender

God as our Constant Companion leads naturally to this next name—our Defender: "You prepare a table before me in the presence of my enemies" (Psalm 23:5 NKJV). What does this mean? Basically, it means you can relax even in the battle. You can trust that the Lord is fighting for you and protecting you. You can sit down and enjoy your meal while He guards you against harm.

The Hebrew name for this name of God is *Jehovah-Nissi*. You are able to relax because He is always protecting you from harm. Right now, thousands of US troops remain deployed at various locations around the world as the war on terror continues. Each hour of every day, these brave men and women sacrifice and serve so that the millions of us back here in our country can enjoy our lives. We can be here without being on alert because we have others watching our backs.

Spiritually, groups of intercessors cover me and everything our church does in prayer practically around the clock. They are our watchers on the wall, praying and keeping the Enemy away from us as we partner with God to advance His kingdom. These two illustrations cannot fully convey the way God is fighting for you right now. "But the Lord is faithful, and he will strengthen you and protect you from the evil one" (2 Thessalonians 3:3 NIV).

God not only defends you but prepares a table where you can be nourished. Your enemies can't touch you as you feed on the goodness of the Lord because He's covering you and fighting for you.

You Are My Sanctifier

The final name of God emerging in this psalm is our Sanctifier: "You anoint my head with oil; my cup runs over" (Psalm 23:5 NKJV). The literal Hebrew name is *Jehovah-M'Kaddesh*, meaning God sets you apart for His special purpose. God has anointed you so that you belong to Him for His sacred use. And He has given you more than you need—your cup runs over—so that you can minister and give to others.

God anoints you so you can use your blessings to bless those around you. He always gives you more than you need so that your generosity can point back to His. "But you are a chosen people, a royal priesthood, a holy nation, God's special possession, that you may declare the praises of him who called you out of darkness into his wonderful light" (1 Peter 2:9 NIV). In Old Testament times, only a select few were trained and anointed to be priests in the temple. But after Jesus, our ultimate High Priest, came and sacrificed Himself for us, we now share in His royal priesthood.

You are called and have a holy purpose. God has not only called you to serve Him as His anointed, but He has also equipped you with His Spirit and unlimited supernatural power. Through Christ, you have everything—and more—you need to do the mission God created you to complete. "May the God of peace, who through the blood of the eternal covenant brought back from the dead our Lord Jesus, that great Shepherd of the sheep, *equip you with everything good for doing his will*, and may he work in us what is pleasing to him, through Jesus Christ, to whom be glory forever and ever. Amen" (Hebrews 13:20–21 NIV, emphasis added).

As you can see, praying all the names of God found in Psalm 23 carries enormous spiritual weight. Without a doubt, it's one of the most powerful ways to pray. When we pray the Prayer of the Sheep, we focus on God and His character—not ourselves, our needs, and our requests. It may seem counterintuitive, but our needs are met as we let go of them and focus completely on who God is in all His glorious dimensions.

After all, God is not answering prayers based on what you've done or who you are. He answers prayers based on who He is. And when you pray this, the outcome is clear: surely goodness and mercy will follow you all the days of your life!

ten

the prayers for the lost

The measure of our love for others can largely be determined by the frequency and earnestness of our prayers for them.

—A. W. Pink

Pastor Chris, you know that Life Saver I've been carrying around in my pocket for months? This afternoon, I got to eat it!" The excitement in my friend's voice sounded like she had just won the lottery. "Peppermint never tasted so good!"

"Praise God! I'm so happy for you," I said. "You've had that Life Saver with you for a long time. Thank you so much for letting me know."

Now before you wonder which one, or both, of us is crazy, let me explain. I'm convinced one of the most important ways we can pray is when we pray for those who do not know the Lord. So at our church, I mention this frequently and our team comes up with creative ways to help people make praying for the lost a prayer priority.

Perhaps the primary way we do this is by regularly distributing prayer cards the size of standard business cards that are blank except for a dozen numbered blanks. We encourage people to jot down the names or initials of twelve people they know who do not yet know Jesus. These individuals often include family members and friends, neighbors and coworkers, cashiers and waitresses, doctors and dentists, pet groomers, and manicurists—anyone you see regularly and interact with on an ongoing basis. Sometimes, it may include someone you met only once.

By putting them on our prayer cards, we commit to praying each day for them to experience God and to accept the free gift of salvation through Jesus Christ. We are intentional about not adorning these little cards with Bible verses, crosses, or the name of our church so that their purpose would not be realized if one of those individuals happened to see it.

We do this for two reasons. First, we don't want anyone who doesn't know Jesus to ever feel like we're being judgmental or self-righteous. And secondly, we never want them to feel like they're a "project." Relationships and prayer are our part in helping them see God accurately and come to know Christ. The Holy Spirit does the rest.

In addition to our prayer cards, we occasionally give out

individually wrapped Life Savers candy and encourage people to keep one in their pocket as a reminder to pray for the people they know who need God. Then, when their prayers are answered, they can eat that Life Saver and begin praying for someone else. So my friend's call was to inform me that her neighbor, whom she'd been praying would accept Jesus, finally invited Him into her life!

There's nothing special about using our prayer cards or carrying around candy. It's simply a matter of whatever works to remind you to be deliberate and consistent in your prayers for others to experience Jesus. Because one of our greatest priorities when we pray should be to lift up those we know and love who need God in their lives.

Ask God to Draw Them to Jesus

God desires everyone to know Him. He loves His creation and wants to enjoy an intimate relationship with each of us. And those who are far from Him weigh heavy on His heart. Jesus said, "If a man owns a hundred sheep, and one of them wanders away, will he not leave the ninety-nine on the hills and go to look for the one that wandered off? And if he finds it, truly I tell you, he is happier about that one sheep than about the ninety-nine that did not wander off" (Matthew 18:12–13 NIV).

As followers of Christ, we're called to partner with Him by praying for these lost sheep who have wandered from the flock. How can we make praying for the lost a regular part of our daily prayers?

There are many ways we can pray for those who need the Lord, but allow me to share the five ways I frequently pray for others.

First, we can ask our Father to draw those individuals to Jesus. God draws people to Him: "No one can come to me unless the Father who sent me draws them" (John 6:44 NIV). This is not something we can make happen based on our own efforts, but we can pray faithfully that our heavenly Father would draw those people He has placed on our hearts to Jesus.

While it's great to pray for all lost people to come to know Christ, we can focus our prayers more fruitfully by praying for those God has placed in our lives. Have you ever had the name of a new acquaintance or someone you see from time to time pop into your mind while you were praying? Sometimes you may not even know anything about your neighbor's, book club friend's, or hair stylist's relationship with God, but you feel this compelling urge to pray for them. Whether or not you share this with them depends on the kind of relationship you have, the context of your interactions, and how you feel led by the Holy Spirit.

You can also simply pay attention to those around you. You can learn a lot about what someone believes just by what they say and how they interact with you. Again, this isn't about judging them—it's about loving them. And sometimes you can tell that they're seeking something more in their lives—more substance, more meaning, more purpose.

As you begin thinking about who you suspect may be far from God, pray for the Spirit to give you wisdom and discernment about how to reflect the Lord's love, grace, and kindness to them. Open your heart and ask God to bring to mind those people you know who need Him. Write down their names as a way to keep your focus on praying for them. There's no right or wrong way to pray for God to draw them to Jesus, but here's a way I often pray:

> *Father,*
>
> *I pray for the people around me, including [list specific names], that You would supernaturally draw their hearts to You. Send Your Holy Spirit to them, and give them the desire to give their lives to You. Help them recognize their longing for more in life as a spiritual thirst only You can quench. Open their ears to hear Your voice and to listen to Your Spirit.*
>
> *In the name of Jesus, I pray.*
> *Amen.*

Bind the Spirit That Blinds Their Minds

Frequently, you may see the spiritual need of those you're praying for more clearly than they do. The truth can be right in front of some people, and they still can't see it because something is in the way blocking their view of God. The Bible explains, "The god of this age has blinded the minds of unbelievers, so that they cannot see the light of the gospel that displays the glory of Christ, who is the image of God" (2 Corinthians 4:4 NIV).

When you're praying for someone who needs the Lord, pray that they see Him without any obstacles or distractions. Pray against whatever is in their way so that they can see the light of

God. Pray that they can see God's power and experience His love based on their own encounter with Him and not what anyone else tells them.

As you'll recall from the Lord's Prayer, when we pray we're connecting with God and we're also defending ourselves from the Enemy. In the next chapter, we'll explore ways to pray and fight the devil. For now, though, when you're praying for the lost, remember to pray that they would see through the Enemy's deceits and resist his temptations.

The last thing the Enemy wants is for a lost person to accept God's gift of salvation and begin a personal relationship with Christ. So the devil will pull out all the stops and use everything in his power to confuse, distract, and blind those who need God. Remember, the Enemy knows how to attack our weaknesses, which includes preventing us from seeing who God really is and the power of His truth.

When I pray for the lost, I make sure I call on the name of Jesus to bind the spirit(s) blinding their minds. My prayer often goes something like this:

> *Father, bind the evil spirits that are blinding the minds of the people around me. In the name of Jesus, I pray that they would be able to see clearly, recognize who You are, and give their hearts to You. Remove all hindrances the Enemy would use to distract them from Your truth. Open their eyes, Lord, that they might see Jesus.*
>
> *In His name, I pray.*
> *Amen.*

Pray for Their Personal Relationship with God

Many people seem to believe Christianity is just another religion. They only see God through the lens of the organization and institution of the church. They may even feel frustrated, angry, or betrayed by people in churches they've encountered or the ones in which they grew up. Others may be turned off by the hypocrisy of religious legalists they've met or seen online.

But Jesus didn't come to build an organization. He came to build a family.

He came to have a *personal relationship* with God's children.

When we invite Jesus into our lives and welcome His Spirit to dwell in us, we begin experiencing the kind of joy, peace, and intimacy we can only know in our relationship with God. We're told, "The Spirit you received does not make you slaves, so that you live in fear again; rather, the Spirit you received brought about your adoption to sonship. And by him we cry, 'Abba, Father'" (Romans 8:15 NIV).

God wants His beloved sons and daughters to come home. Praying for people to have personal encounters with the living God makes a huge difference. They realize that God is not an angry judge waiting to punish them but a loving Father unlike anyone they've ever met. They are no longer blinded by misconceptions about God, because they have begun to see the truth of who He is for themselves.

When I pray for people to know the Lord, I usually pray like this:

Father,

I pray that people will understand how much You love them. Loose the spirit of adoption for the people around me so that they can come into a meaningful relationship with You. Stir in their hearts a longing to come home, to hear Your voice, and to see You welcoming them with open arms. Let them know You are always running to meet them and hold them close. In the name of Jesus, amen.

Pray for Believers to Cross Their Paths

Have you ever noticed how God often brings the right people into our lives at just the right time? When we pray for others to join the family of God, it helps to pray for them to encounter as many followers of Jesus as possible.

The reason is twofold. We can pray for other Christians to influence the people around them positively, and we can also look for opportunities to influence others positively ourselves. God's plan to reach people is worked out through those who already know and love Him. Jesus asked us to pray for people to be sent into the world to be salt and light (Matthew 5:13–16). Christ came to bring the good news of the gospel to all people, and He desires that everyone should know and love Him. "Ask the Lord of the harvest, therefore, to send out workers into his harvest field" (Matthew 9:38 NIV).

As God's "spiritual farmers," we should be attuned to opportunities to plant spiritual seeds in the lives of the people we encounter each day. We may have no idea who has already been praying for them and the cumulative impact our kind words, compassionate acts, or loving attitudes can have in drawing them to Christ. As we grow in our faith and draw closer to God, we naturally want to share who He is with everyone around us.

Being sensitive to others' spiritual needs does not mean preaching or quoting Scripture. It means showing kindness, patience, and a willingness to help without expecting anything in return. God usually reveals Himself to the lost through those who already love and serve Him. When praying for the lost to be surrounded by believers, you might pray similar to this:

Father,

I pray for the lost around me to meet believers who will influence them in a positive way. Lord, let my life shine in such a way that people will want to know the God I serve. Allow others to see my genuine love and concern for them in all that I say and do. Let me be Your hands and feet to serve them, and let them know just how much You love them.

In Jesus' name, amen.

Release the Spirit of Wisdom and Revelation

Everyone reaches a moment of spiritual revelation in their own way. Many people reach it when their world gets turned upside down by unexpected circumstances or painful losses. They

Being sensitive to others' spiritual needs does not mean preaching or quoting Scripture. It means showing kindness, patience, and a willingness to help without anything in return.

realize they simply cannot move forward in their lives without God. Others pursue wealth, success, and achievement only to discover that nothing is ever enough. They still long for something only a relationship with God can fill.

When they open their heart, it suddenly clicks. They experience a kind of spiritual "aha!" moment when God's presence is real to them like never before. When the spiritual light comes on, they recognize their sin, see what Jesus did on the cross, and accept the hope that comes from giving their life to God. "I keep asking that the God of our Lord Jesus Christ, the glorious Father, may give the Spirit of wisdom and revelation, so that you may know him better" (Ephesians 1:17 NIV).

People need wisdom, not just knowledge of spiritual things and insight into how spiritual realities directly impact them. We can pray for this kind of supernatural revelation that only comes from God:

Father,

I pray for the people around me to experience the spirit of wisdom and revelation. I pray that they would truly understand their spiritual condition and see the debt Jesus paid for them on the cross. Help them have the information and experiences needed to come to You, so they can understand all You have for them.
In the name of Jesus, I pray. Amen.

Praying for the lost to come home to God requires patience on our part. We can relay all kinds of information, give away Bibles or share apps, quote Scripture and what famous theologians say about it. But nothing we do can draw another human being to God like prayer. Incorporating our prayers for the lost into our regular prayer practice keeps them on our minds and hearts.

Nothing we do can draw another human being to God like prayer. Incorporating our prayers for the lost into our regular prayer practice keeps them on our minds and hearts.

You've likely heard numerous testimonies of the impact prayer has had on individual lives. Grandparents praying for grandchildren, parents praying for prodigals, friends praying for classmates, teachers praying for students, coaches praying for players, and acquaintances praying for people they met only one time. God wants everyone everywhere to know Him and experience the freedom that comes from Christ. There may be no better way to love another person than to pray for them to know the Lord!

eleven

the prayers for warfare

_____

Satan laughs at our toil, mocks at our
wisdom, but trembles when we pray.

—Samuel Chadwick

A friend of mine recently asked me to pray for him, specifically to pray for power and victory over the Enemy's assaults in his life. He was working with me on a new ministry project and knew this immediately made him a high-profile target for the devil. He had become more aware of how the Enemy operates.

"It's become conspicuous," he said. "Just a lot of little things— problems, conflicts, distractions. I thank God that there's no major crisis going on, but the number of interruptions is staggering. Sort of death by paper cuts. At first I thought I might be imagining it, but now it's pretty clear that the Enemy doesn't like what I'm doing."

"You're not imagining things," I told him. "What you're working on can have a huge impact for God's kingdom and strengthen the faith of countless believers—the last thing the devil wants to happen. So I'll be happy to pray for you and will ask my prayer intercessors to pray for you as well."

I've come to expect the devil to interfere with what's going on around me. I've always had a healthy respect for the temptations and trials posed by dark spiritual forces. But early in my ministry I discovered that certain things tend to go wrong the more I'm moving in the right direction—especially when my words and actions can reflect who God is to those around me.

More Than Meets the Eye

One of the examples I've shared often occurred shortly after we started Church of the Highlands. My daughter, Sarah, then thirteen, suffered painful irritation in one of her eyes, resulting in doctors' visits indicating that Sarah could lose her vision, which might be a precursor to multiple sclerosis. My wife, Tammy, and I were stunned. In addition, Sarah's struggles "just happened" to coincide with our church's first big outreach to the community. This revelation caused me to pray like never before, asking God to heal Sarah, to give wisdom to Tammy and me, and to protect us from the Enemy's attacks.

The Lord answered my prayers quickly. A friend at church sent us to see her father, a neurologist, and get his opinion on Sarah's condition. He ran tests and assured us that Sarah did not have MS and encouraged us to give her distressed eye a few more days to heal on its own. Which, in fact, it did—the day *after* we successfully held our outreach! Sarah's vision returned to normal, and she's had no trouble with her eyes since then.

Sarah's mysterious eye ailment confirmed my belief in the unseen spiritual realities around us. If this sort of situation had happened only once, I might be tempted to wonder if I was reading too much into it. After more than four decades as a Christian and nearly that long as a pastor, though, I know without a doubt the Enemy works hard to undermine God's people.

Nearly every year right before Easter weekend, just as we're about to welcome record numbers of visitors at multiple services throughout Alabama, something happens—a calamity, conflict, or crisis out of the blue. During the week of our Christmas services, another time when we experience thousands of visitors at our services, the same kind of distractions, disturbances, and diversions occur. The same goes whenever I have a new book about to release or when I'm about to lead a conference for thousands of pastors.

These numerous experiences aren't the reason I believe in spiritual warfare, though. God's Word is the reason I know the Enemy has us in his sights. The Bible reveals that an invisible spiritual dimension is always operating around us, which the apostle Paul called the "heavenly realms." There, according to Paul, a battle rages: "For our struggle is not against flesh and blood, but against the rulers, against the authorities, against the powers of this dark world and against the spiritual forces of evil in the heavenly realms" (Ephesians 6:12 NIV).

Why pray prayers of warfare?

To confront the Enemy with the power of God!

Enemy Lines

We are far from defenseless, however. You'll recall that prayer is not only communion with God—it is confrontation with the Enemy. Confronting him and accessing God's power to overcome

Spiritual warfare is not an option—it's an essential part of growing in your faith and living victoriously.

the devil must be foundational to your prayer times. Spiritual warfare is not an option—it's an essential part of growing in your faith and living victoriously.

Don't worry if praying and engaging in spiritual warfare is new and unfamiliar to you. Perhaps you've heard the term but dismissed it as too extreme or irrelevant to your own prayer life. I promise, though, including prayers of warfare is essential to experiencing the victory you have in Christ. I don't want you to be frightened or overly alarmed, but I do want you to take warfare seriously. Because if you don't, you automatically give the Enemy extra leverage in your life.

We need to keep three points in mind regarding our antagonist in spiritual warfare. First and foremost, *the devil is real.* Don't make the mistake of assuming he's imaginary, mythical, fictional, or harmless. One of his greatest tricks is convincing people that he doesn't exist.

Next, *the devil wants to destroy you*: "The thief comes only to steal and kill and destroy" (John 10:10 NIV). The Enemy constantly schemes and plots ways he can rob us of our joy, peace, and purpose, which is why we must take him seriously and engage in warfare through our prayers. Peter warned us, "Be alert and of sober mind. Your enemy the devil prowls around like a roaring lion looking for someone to devour. Resist him, standing firm in the faith" (1 Peter 5:8–9 NIV).

The third and final point to remember is that *the devil is limited*. Yes, the Bible describes demonic beings as "authorities" over certain worldly powers that they wield against us, but their authority has a limit. Simply put, demons yield to God and submit to His authority. They tremble at the name of Jesus. God's Word promises us, "The one who is in you is greater than the one who is in the world" (1 John 4:4 NIV).

Prayer Armor

During His time on earth, Jesus showed us how to handle our confrontations with the devil. Shortly after being baptized, Jesus went into the wilderness to fast and pray and square off against the Evil One (Matthew 4; Luke 4). Three times the Enemy tried to tempt Christ, and each time Jesus responded by drawing on Scripture. He showed us how to use the sword of truth, the Word of God, to defend ourselves from the devil's attacks. Christ's example demonstrates how we, too, can experience victory over the Enemy's assaults.

There are a number of spiritual warfare prayers we can adapt from Scripture when we or someone we know is under attack from the devil. Knowing that we are in a spiritual battle, God provides spiritual armor and equips us to take a stand when battles come our way. Based on Ephesians 6, take up the protection God has given you by praying through the different pieces of armor described in the following passage:

> Put on the full armor of God, so that you can take your stand against the devil's schemes. For our struggle is not against flesh and blood, but against the rulers, against the authorities, against the powers of this dark world and against the spiritual forces of evil in the heavenly realms. Therefore put on the full armor of God, so that when the day of evil comes, you may be able to stand your ground, and after you have done everything, to stand. Stand firm then, with the belt of truth buckled around your waist, with the breastplate of righteousness in place, and with your feet fitted with the readiness that comes from the gospel of peace. In addition to all this, take up the shield of faith, with which you can extinguish all the flaming arrows of the evil one. Take the helmet of salvation and the sword of the Spirit, which is the word of God.
>
> And pray in the Spirit on all occasions with all kinds of

prayers and requests. With this in mind, be alert and always keep on praying for all the Lord's people. (Ephesians 6:11–18 NIV)

As you pray through this preparation for spiritual battle, I encourage you to make it your own. Here's the prayer I like to use based on this passage:

Thank You, Lord, for my salvation. I receive it in a new and fresh way from You, and I declare that nothing can separate me from the love of Christ and the place I have in Your kingdom. I wear Your righteousness today against all condemnation and corruption. Cover me with Your holiness and purity—defend me from all attacks against my heart.

Lord, I put on the belt of truth. I choose a lifestyle of honesty and integrity. Expose the lies I have believed, and show me Your truth today. I choose to live for the gospel in every moment. Show me where You are working and lead me to it. Give me strength to walk daily with You. I believe that You are powerful against every lie and attack of the Enemy, and I receive and claim Your power in my life. Nothing is coming today that can overcome me because You are with me. Holy Spirit, show me the truths of the Word of God that I will need to counter the traps of the Enemy. Bring those scriptures to mind today. Finally, Holy Spirit, I agree to walk in step with You in everything as my spirit communes with You in prayer throughout the day.

Word of Truth

When we are aware of spiritual warfare, we can be active in praying through it. God has given us victory and power to fight through the blood of Christ. We can overcome anything that comes against the truth of God and His Word by calling on the name of Jesus. The Bible tells us:

> Therefore God exalted him to the highest place and gave him the name that is above every name, that at the name of Jesus every knee should bow, in heaven and on earth and under the earth, and every tongue acknowledge that Jesus Christ is Lord, to the glory of God the Father. (Philippians 2:9–11 NIV)

Empowered and protected by Christ's authority, you must take a bold stand, praying specifically and confidently through God's power and His Spirit. Receive the spiritual power that comes from the authority of the living God you serve and use it to overcome the Enemy's advances.

Once again, you should pray in a way that reflects your relationship with God and the situations you're currently facing. The prayer I use focuses on the power of God's Word and the power of the name of Jesus:

> *Father, Your Word says that no weapon formed against me will prosper (Isaiah 54:17), and I declare it in Jesus' name. Your Word says that trouble will not arise a second time (Nahum 1:9). So I declare in Jesus' name that Satan cannot*

We can overcome
anything that comes
against the truth of
God and His Word
by calling on the
name of Jesus.

make trouble for me again, like he has in the past. I declare in the name of Jesus that all of these prayers are answered and taken care of by trusting You.

I stand on Your Word. The Enemy is driven out from me and from my home, workplace, church family, children, and loved ones. I declare that he is not able to stand against me. No weapon formed against me will prosper, because the Spirit of the Lord is with me, protecting me. I declare these truths in the name of Jesus. Anything that comes against me or my family that is not in line with the truth and will of God, I command to bow to the powerful name of Jesus. Father God, I give You all of my thanksgiving, praise, glory, honor, and worship. Thank You for loving me, making me clean, and giving me purpose.

Prayer of Protection

When we confront the Enemy in spiritual warfare—and even when we don't, for that matter—we often worry about our safety and protection. We feel vulnerable and wonder when and how the devil may try to attack us. When we feel this way, we can immediately come to God in prayer, pouring out our hearts to Him, and battling in the heavenlies by asking for and claiming protection for ourselves and our families in Jesus' name. God's Word assures us that He will always empower and protect us: "But the Lord is faithful, and he will strengthen you and protect you from the evil one" (2 Thessalonians 3:3 NIV).

Whether you're feeling worried or not, share your thoughts and concerns with God. Ask Him for His supernatural protection. He says He will command His angels concerning you to guard you in all your ways (Psalm 91:11). Trust this promise and lay everything down before Him, trusting His good plans and His power to protect you and those you love. Drawing on several different New Testament passages (Romans 12:1–2; 2 Corinthians 6:14–7:1; 10:3–5; 2 Thessalonians 3:3), I like to pray the following prayer of protection:

God, I bow in worship to praise You. Thank You for making a way for me through Your Son, Jesus. I surrender myself completely in every area of my life to You. I submit myself to the true and living God and refuse any involvement of the Enemy in my life. I choose to be transformed by the renewing of my mind. I reject every thought that tries to compete against the knowledge of Christ. I pray and thank You for a sound mind, the mind of Christ.

Today and every day I ask for protection over my family and loved ones—all immediate family members, relatives, friends, acquaintances, and myself. I ask for protection during all our travels. I ask You to watch over our financial security, possessions, health, and safety [be as specific here as you like]. All that I have is Yours, God, and I declare that Satan cannot touch me or anything You have given me. I

*rebuke the Enemy and tell him to bow to the blood of Jesus
that covers me and my family. He will not take what You
have given us, and we are protected and provided for by
You, God, and You alone.*

In Jesus' name I pray, amen.

Winning the War

When you engage in prayers of warfare, it's helpful to keep three
key strategies in mind. First and foundational to your efforts, *you
must daily submit yourself to God.* Your ability to fight the devil is
only as strong as your relationship with the Lord. His Word urges,
"Submit yourselves, then, to God. Resist

Your ability to fight the devil is only as strong as your relationship with the Lord.

the devil, and he will flee from you"
(James 4:7 NIV). Don't miss the sequence
here: First you submit to God, and then
you resist the devil. And then watch him
flee! Think of this process of submission
and resistance as recharging your spiritual battery. Your relationship with God
gives you power and authority. When you surrender yourself to
Christ daily, you walk by faith in the power of the Holy Spirit.

After submitting to God, the second key is to *resist the
Enemy by closing any doors in your life that give him access.* If
you leave your doors and windows open and unlocked in your
home, you might as well extend an invitation for others to rob
you. Burglars don't need to break in because you've made it

easy for them. Similarly, don't leave yourself open to the dark thief.

When you disobey God, ignore His commandments, and yield to temptation, you give the devil an open door into your life. One wide-open door we often overlook is unforgiveness. Forgiving others and seeking forgiveness are essential to our spiritual security system. Paul explained, "Anyone you forgive, I also forgive. And what I have forgiven—if there was anything to forgive—I have forgiven in the sight of Christ for your sake, in order that Satan might not outwit us. For we are not unaware of his schemes" (2 Corinthians 2:10–11 NIV).

Notice Paul's warning here: when we fail to forgive, we create an opening for the devil to enter with his schemes. This provides extra incentive to make sure we are right before God and with the people in our lives. As part of your prayer time, I encourage you to include confession and forgiveness. One prayer I like to use is this one:

Lord,

I have a confession to make. I haven't loved others well. I have resented certain people and have not forgiven them in my heart. God, I know that You have forgiven me for so much, and I need Your help to follow You and forgive others. In faith, I now forgive [name them]. I also forgive and accept myself because You have made me new in the name of Jesus. In His name I pray, amen.

Paul also warned, "'In your anger do not sin': Do not let the sun go down while you are still angry, and do not give the devil a foothold" (Ephesians 4:26–27 NIV). Paul knew that the Enemy likes to take advantage of us when we allow our emotions to get the best of us. When our feelings overwhelm us and cloud our judgment, the devil loves to seize any opening in our defenses.

All the more reason to practice spiritual warfare with your prayers, which points us to our third defensive key—*confronting the Enemy every day.* Your spiritual confrontation should include exposing the devil's lies because lying is what he does best: "When he lies, he speaks his native language, for he is a liar and the father of lies" (John 8:44 NIV). Exposing his lies is vitally important because a lie believed as truth will affect your life as if it were true. And when we expose the lie, we defeat the liar.

We confront the Enemy every day by claiming God's truth. That's what Jesus did. Jesus used the Word of God as His weapon to fight the Enemy and so should we. When we know the truth, the truth sets us free (John 8:32). How does knowing and living in truth free us? By providing a supernatural weapon against what we allow to take root in our lives, minds, and hearts. God's Word instructs us:

> For though we live in the world, we do not wage war as the world does. The weapons we fight with are not the weapons of the world. On the contrary, they have divine power to demolish strongholds. We demolish arguments and every pretension that sets itself up against the knowledge of God, and we take captive every thought to make it obedient to Christ. (2 Corinthians 10:3–5 NIV)

The Greek word translated "strongholds" in this passage is *ochyroma*, which literally refers to a prisoner locked up by deception. When you're trapped in a stronghold, you're living life based on something that's not true. A stronghold is not big enough or powerful enough to stop us, but we think it is.

This false assumption reminds me of the fable about the circus elephant who was restrained only by a thin rope. The trainers started by using a heavy chain when the elephant was young. After enough unsuccessful attempts to break free, the elephant simply stopped trying to escape. From then on, only a light rope was required to keep the animal in its pen. Even though it could have easily snapped the rope if it tried, it assumed it was still bound by the unbreakable chain.

The devil operates the same way with us. He has power but no authority. So he keeps talking to us and lying until we believe the lie instead of the truth. Consequently, everything that exalts itself in our minds is a pretension. Satan pretends that he has authority over us and, as the father of lies (John 8:44), he's very good at his job. But through Christ, we have God's authority to break free of these lies and live in the truth.

When you filter your thoughts by making them captive to your knowledge of God and obedience to Christ, you're empowered to "violently cast down" such strongholds. "Violently cast down" is the literal meaning of the Greek word *kathaireo*, translated here as "demolish." Imagine breaking through the walls of deception by focusing on God's truth. We have the authority and power to cast out fallen angels—if we're willing to engage in warfare.

No matter how you feel or what you're going through, you have access to the power of the living God. His Spirit dwells in you and provides strength, stamina, and the power you need to overcome the Enemy's attacks and live victoriously in Christ. He has won the battle already so you don't have to rely on your own abilities. You simply need to access His power and confront the Enemy each day as you learn to pray first!

twelve

the prayer for you

Prayer does not fit us for the greater
works; prayer *is* the greater work.

—Oswald Chambers

The "salt pan" in Death Valley, located in eastern California, is the hottest, driest place in the United States. Along with deserts in the Middle East and the Sahara, this desolate area in Death Valley is one of the most extreme places in the world. Its parched, arid surface prevents anything from growing there continuously. No trees, no bushes, no flowers or plants—nothing. Which explains why no one lives there—it's simply not feasible for homes, businesses, and the infrastructure needed to sustain them.

Occasionally, once or twice a decade, there's significant rainfall on the salt flats of Death Valley. In fact, in 2015, a year's worth of rain fell in a relatively short amount of time. With no ground cover to hold the rainwater, it washed the clay-like surface clean. But then the following spring, in 2016, the barren ground sprouted tiny green shoots. Then wildflowers began to bloom. And not just two or three—within a couple weeks a carpet of wildflowers blanketed most of the valley in a stunning display of red, yellow, and light blue blossoms.

This natural phenomenon is called a "super bloom" and occurs on average about once a decade. In addition to being an unbelievable spectacle of God's creation, these super blooms prove that life is indeed possible in Death Valley—but only when the conditions are right. Apparently, those wildflower seeds lay dormant beneath the terra-cotta–baked soil, just waiting to be watered enough to sprout and bloom.

I love seeing the before-and-after photos of the Death Valley super blooms because they remind us that if the conditions are right, life will happen. Something—or someone—that seems dead and hopeless can be resurrected into blossoming with supernatural beauty. I can think of no better picture of how we can flourish in our faith when we experience the right conditions for spiritual growth. The psalmist tells us, "Those who are planted in the house of the LORD shall flourish in the courts of our God" (Psalm 92:13 NKJV).

No matter where you are in life or in your journey of faith, you can experience the fullness of what God wants to give you. And prayer, of course, is an instrumental part of the process.

I Keep Asking

God has made it clear throughout the Bible that there's a path to life that produces fruit, fulfillment, and joy. You see it in this prayer by the apostle Paul, someone who knew a thing or two about dramatic transformations:

> I have not stopped giving thanks for you, remembering you in my prayers. I keep asking that the God of our Lord Jesus Christ, the glorious Father, may give you the Spirit of wisdom and revelation, so that you may know him better. I pray that the eyes of your heart may be enlightened in order that you may know the hope to which he has called you, the riches of his glorious inheritance in his holy people, and his incomparably great power for us who believe. (Ephesians 1:16–19 NIV)

I love these verses. This has become a prayer that I pray every day for the people I shepherd. Clearly, this prayer was one Paul prayed frequently as well—he said, "I keep asking." And I pray the same four parts that Paul outlined for us here: to know God better, to know the hope to which God calls us, to experience the glorious inheritance in His holy people, and to be conduits of His great power to change the world. In order to make them memorable and more accessible, I like to summarize them like this:

- Know God
- Find freedom
- Discover purpose
- Make a difference

In fact, these four elements not only summarize our progression as we walk with God—they serve as our foundation for virtually everything we do at Church of the Highlands. These four components cover what I like to call the Christian continuum, the growth cycle we experience when we walk with God and mature in our faith. They reflect the overlapping processes of experiential growth and Christian maturity.

Know God

Notice that Paul's first request is for God to give these followers of Jesus "the Spirit of wisdom and revelation." And for what purpose? "So that you may know him better." Simply put, Paul wanted these believers to know God and grow in their knowledge of Him. Our relationship with God is fundamental to all the other progressive stages. Knowing Him is an ongoing process over our lifetimes, not a one-time memorization of facts or theology. Our relationship with Him anchors us no matter our circumstances or life seasons.

Knowing God in this sense is not necessarily about mere knowledge—knowing *about* Him. I know about the British monarchy and some facts about Queen Elizabeth II, but I don't have a relationship with her that affords me firsthand experience of who she is and what she's like. Knowing in this basic sense is often from a distance, detached and objective.

The kind of knowing Paul referenced in this passage refers to a personal, experiential, intimate relationship with God. The Greek word is *ginosko*, which was influenced heavily by the Hebrew word *yada*, found in the Old Testament as a polite euphemism for the way a husband and wife know one another, including sexually. Adam *knew* Eve and she became pregnant (Genesis 4:1). This is the kind of intense closeness we experience when we begin a spiritual relationship with our Creator.

Everything starts with knowing God, with your authentic relationship with the three persons of the Godhead. I pray that everyone I serve will know Him—Father, Son, and Holy Spirit—and experience the fullness of who He is. For those who already know Him, I pray that they will grow to have a deeper, fuller, richer relationship with the Lord. Knowing God is paramount to all other aspects of our spiritual lives. Jesus reinforced this truth by indicating that not everyone claiming to know Him actually does:

> "Not everyone who says to me, 'Lord, Lord,' will enter the kingdom of heaven, but only the one who does the will of my Father who is in heaven. Many will say to me on that day, 'Lord, Lord, did we not prophesy in your name and in your name drive out demons and in your name perform many miracles?' Then I

will tell them plainly, 'I never knew you. Away from me, you evildoers!'" (Matthew 7:21–23 NIV)

Knowing God should be our priority—not learning about Him or even serving others in His name, but spending time with Him, praising and worshiping, talking and listening. The more we get to know Him, the more we want to know.

Find Freedom

Once your relationship with God is underway, your spiritual growth is about finding freedom. Returning to Paul's prayer in Ephesians, we find, "I ask—ask the God of our Master, Jesus Christ, the God of glory—to make you intelligent and discerning in knowing him personally, *your eyes focused and clear, so that you can see exactly what it is he is calling you to do*" (Ephesians 1:17–18, THE MESSAGE, emphasis added). Or considering the NIV, it reads, "I pray that the eyes of your heart may be enlightened in order that you may know the hope to which he has called you" (Ephesians 1:18 NIV).

I love that phrase "the eyes of your heart" because the greatest gift I can give others when I pray this prayer, and certainly when I preach, is clarity. When you have spiritual clarity based on knowing God, you discover what your purpose is, what you're called to do, how you should live, and how to grow in your faith.

In order to have clarity, though, your heart-lens must be clean and clear. Your heart is a filter for how you see things in

Knowing God should be our priority—not learning about Him or even serving others in His name, but spending time with Him, praising and worshiping, talking and listening. The more we get to know Him, the more we want to know.

life—your hurts, wounds, trials and triumphs, experiences both good and bad. We're told, "Keep your heart with all diligence, for out of it spring the issues of life" (Proverbs 4:23 NKJV). In other words, keep your heart-filter clean because it holds the issues of life.

Indeed, our hearts do get clogged up at times, which means we must get rid of the dirt and pollution clouding our spiritual vision. Because if you don't see clearly, you will miss the hope to which God has called you. If you don't get heart-clear, you're missing the calling He has on your life—the unique purpose for which you were created.

But to discover and live out your purpose, you must overcome the sins that entangle you and hold you back. The Bible is clear about how this is accomplished: "Therefore confess your sins to each other and pray for each other so that you may be healed" (James 5:16 NIV). Many don't understand this necessity, and some don't like the process when they do understand.

But we all have issues—if you don't think you have issues, that's your issue! So we all need to be in a community with other followers of Jesus where we can be known, do life together, and encourage one another in our faith. "Let us think of ways to motivate one another to acts of love and good works. And let us not neglect our meeting together, as some people do, but encourage one another, especially now that the day of his return is drawing near" (Hebrews 10:24–25 NLT). Confession with other believers requires vulnerability and trust. But as soon as you confess your faults one to another and pray for one another, the Bible promises healing.

At Church of the Highlands, this requires getting involved in a small group. We have several thousand small groups going at any one time. Regardless of what the groups are focused around—marriage, parenting, debt and finances, volleyball, books, Bible study, whatever—the goal is to build relationships and help one another see clearly so that we all may grow stronger in our faith.

The more our church has grown, the more deliberately we've focused on our small groups to ensure everyone is connecting in meaningful community. Because any church is too big if you don't know anybody! A big church becomes small and personal once you're part of a group of like-minded believers focused on experiencing the freedom we have in Christ.

Discover Purpose

Once you've found freedom and experienced victory over your big issues, then you can discover your purpose and live out the calling God has placed on your life. You can't discover purpose if you haven't found freedom.

Many people don't see their God-given purpose because they're limited by the cloudy lens they're using. When you see clearly and find your calling, it brings hope to your life. Other than the day you were born, the two most important days in your life are the day you are born again and the day you figure out why you were born. Without clarity, you miss out on the journey of joy that God wants to take you on.

Everyone has God-given gifts that are unique to you and your journey. God's Word says, "We have different gifts, according to the grace given to each of us" (Romans 12:6 NIV). The original Greek word here for "gifts," or literally "grace gifts," is *charis*—the same root from which we get the words *charisma* and *charismatic*. "God has given each of you a gift from his great variety of spiritual gifts. Use them well to serve one another" (1 Peter 4:10 NLT).

When people ask me if our church is charismatic, I make sure they realize that every church, comprised of *charis*-using believers, should be charismatic in this way. But usually they're referring to cultural stereotypes of snake-handling and other practices that are definitely *not* part of what we do!

Discovering and utilizing your gifts requires exploring how God made you. At Highlands we have a series of classes called the "Growth Track" that helps people do this through a variety of different assessments and personality-revealing resources. We want to help people identify ways to serve that align with their gifts and passions. Allow me to emphasize again that everyone has different gifts.

You may be thrilled to make sure that all the chairs are straight when setting up for your church's services. Or perhaps you have a heart for children and a gift for teaching and mentoring them. You might love exercising hospitality and hosting events, making sure everyone feels included and appreciated. Business acumen and financial stewardship might come naturally to you. Or your compassionate heart for others may draw you to serve the community at a clinic, shelter, or food bank.

God has given all of us different gifts—but we have to know what they are in order to use them. "Now about the gifts of the Spirit, brothers and sisters, I do not want you to be uninformed" (1 Corinthians 12:1 NIV). Too many people are ignorant of their *charis*-abilities. This has to change if you want to live the full, abundant life God has for you!

Too many people are ignorant of their *charis*-abilities. This has to change if you want to live the full, abundant life God has for you!

Make a Difference

This brings us to the fourth and final progressive stage—exercising your gifts for God's glory and the advancement of His kingdom. Making an eternal difference is the ultimate fulfillment—your life, joined with the rest of the saints, creating a holy impact for eternity.

That's the best there is! This is the greenest pasture for us to experience as God's sheep. He is our Good Shepherd and wants to lead us there, but we have to be willing to trust Him each step of the way.

There's nothing like knowing you're making a positive difference in the lives of others. When you have something in your life worth living for, you discover real joy—and so many of your problems, struggles, and distractions suddenly fall away. Jesus said, "This is to my Father's glory, that you bear much fruit, showing yourselves to be my disciples. . . . I have told you this so that my joy may be in you and that your joy may be complete" (John 15:8, 11 NIV).

Bearing fruit is pleasing to God and reflects His glory—but it also does something in you. Bearing fruit produces joy in you as you live out your purpose and serve others with the unique gifts that God invested in you. You discover the harmony of being part of God's family and living for the only cause that counts—sharing the gospel of Jesus Christ. "All of you together are Christ's body, and each of you is a part of it" (1 Corinthians 12:27 NLT).

What I often call "The Prayer for You" is a prayer not only for yourself but also for all the other believers you know. This concise prayer encompasses the progression of your own growth and the growth of those alongside you as followers of Jesus. Praying this prayer ensures that you remain focused on where you are in your walk with God while providing perspective on the big picture of the Christian life.

You not only pray this prayer—*you live it*!

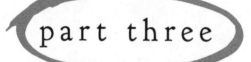

part three

Prayer and Fasting

Have you any days of fasting and prayer?
Storm the throne of grace and persevere
therein, and mercy will come down.

—John Wesley

thirteen

this kind

━━━━━━━━━━

Prayer is reaching out after the unseen; fasting
is letting go of all that is seen and temporal.

—Andrew Murray

The first time I did a serious fast, I was battling depres-
sion. It was 1999 and I had reached a point where I felt stuck, both
as a Christian and as a pastor. I desperately needed clarity and
direction for my life and decided that 21 days of prayer and fasting
would draw me closer to the Lord and jump-start my faith as well
as show me the steps to take for moving forward.

On day 17 I had a vision of me preaching on stage at what I
would later realize was Church of the Highlands. Despite the fear

of preaching to so many people in an unfamiliar place, I knew this was where God wanted to lead me. After my fast ended, I talked with my pastor, and he helped me start the process of planting a church. As I continue to marvel at all the Lord has done and continues to do through Highlands, I always come back to that breakthrough with prayer and fasting.

Ready for More

Many people view fasting as something reserved for hard-core believers in remote places—people so committed to their faith that they've left society behind to focus only on God. Other people consider fasting to be a tradition that's no longer relevant in the twenty-first century. A few might even think fasting is only a trendy way to lose weight and increase health benefits!

At its essence, however, fasting is a fundamental spiritual discipline for anyone—not just monks and nuns, missionaries and pilgrims—seeking more of God. Fasting takes our faith to another level and increases the effectiveness of our prayers. I consider it such a vital part of prayer that I would be failing in my objective in this book without encouraging you to understand and practice fasting as part of your prayer life.

Another reason to practice prayer with fasting is to more fully experience your freedom in Christ. Many people come to me as a pastor because they're struggling in their faith. Some are bound by the power of addiction in their lives—to food, alcohol, drugs, sex, porn, gambling, shopping, or something else. Others simply feel stuck and can't quite put their finger on why they're not grow-ing in their walk with God. Some seek my counsel because they're praying daily, and while they've matured spiritually, they want more—more of God, more of His power, more healing, more joy.

Without judging them, I typically try to get a handle on how to help them by considering the three categories of people described by the apostle Paul in his letter to the early church at Corinth. First, there's the *unspiritual* person. Paul explained, "The person without the Spirit does not accept the things that come from the Spirit of God but considers them foolishness, and cannot understand them because they are discerned only through the Spirit" (1 Corinthians 2:14 NIV). If someone does not know God and have His Spirit dwelling in them, then the place to start is by beginning a personal relationship with Him through the gift of grace available to everyone through Jesus Christ.

Next, Paul described the *spiritual* person—someone already in relationship with God. "The person with the Spirit makes judg-ments about all things, but such a person is not subject to merely human judgments, for 'Who has known the mind of the Lord so as to instruct him?' But we have the mind of Christ" (1 Corinthians 2:15–16 NIV).

Finally, there's what Paul called the *worldly* person—people who know God at a basic level but have not grown or matured in their faith:

> Brothers and sisters, I could not address you as people who live by the Spirit but as people who are still worldly—mere infants in Christ. I gave you milk, not solid food, for you were

not yet ready for it. Indeed, you are still not ready. You are still worldly. For since there is jealousy and quarreling among you, are you not worldly? Are you not acting like mere humans? (1 Corinthians 3:1–3 NIV)

Have you been settling for milk when you crave solid spiritual food?

It's time to consider your spiritual diet.

Free Indeed

No one wants to remain an infant sustained on milk when they can grow and mature and feast on the solid food of the Spirit. It's important to know where you are spiritually so you can have a starting point. If you've been on a diet of spiritual milk for some time, you're likely ready to take your faith to the next level and experience greater intimacy with God. To do this, you need to move past the trap of perpetual sin.

Otherwise, your faith will merely revolve around your mistakes and your need for forgiveness. Throughout life in this fallen world, you will still have moments when you sin and need to ask for forgiveness, but you don't have to stay stuck in a daily rinse-and-repeat cycle. God has so much more for you than that.

Knowing where you are spiritually is the starting point regardless of your struggles. And if you're not struggling, then praise God! You're likely more than ready to take your faith to the next level and experience more intimacy with Him. Because once you enter into relationship with Christ, you can have freedom from the bondage of sin:

> To the Jews who had believed him, Jesus said, "If you hold to my teaching, you are really my disciples. Then you will know the truth, and the truth will set you free."
>
> They answered him, "We are Abraham's descendants and have never been slaves of anyone. How can you say that we shall be set free?"
>
> Jesus replied, "Very truly I tell you, everyone who sins is a slave to sin. Now a slave has no permanent place in the family, but a son belongs to it forever. So if the Son sets you free, you will be free indeed. (John 8:31–36 NIV)

While we have been set free—*free indeed*—by the Son, we remain spiritual beings in a body of flesh. Even though our salvation is secured and the Holy Spirit dwells in us, we are still works in progress capable of making sinful choices—even when we know better and don't want to do so. Paul expressed this frustration in a way we can all relate to at some level: "I do not understand what I do. For what I want to do I do not do, but what I hate I do. . . . For I have the desire to do what is good, but I cannot carry it out" (Romans 7:15, 18 NIV). Paul went on to conclude, "Now if I do what I do not want to do, it is no longer I who do it, but it is sin living in me that does it" (Romans 7:20 NIV).

I'm not sure I've ever heard a better spiritual description of addiction than in the paradox Paul described. Basically, addiction reflects the pattern of doing something you really don't want to do and/or not doing something you really do want to do.

What causes this ongoing tension? The Bible tells us that we are tripart beings comprised of body, soul, and spirit. Because our bodies are the tangible, visible part we see and feel, we tend to let our bodies, including our emotions, rule our hearts—which is why fasting is so essential for refocusing on God and strengthening our spirit. Fasting weakens the body and its appetites so that we can keep our eyes on Jesus. Simply put, fasting is about less of us and more of God.

Simply put, fasting is about less of us and more of God.

In stark contrast to the constant messages in today's society, fasting denies the things that our flesh craves—food, alcohol, and anything we use for pleasure and distraction. When we suppress those cravings and appetites and force our bodies to yield to our spirits, we create space for drawing closer to God and aligning our hearts with His. And when we're aligned with Him, we have full access to His unlimited power through the Holy Spirit, including the power to overcome those stubborn, sinful areas that continue to hold us back in our faith:

> Therefore, dear brothers and sisters, you have no obligation to do what your sinful nature urges you to do. For if you live by its dictates, you will die. But if through the power of the Spirit you put to death the deeds of your sinful nature, you will live. For all who are led by the Spirit of God are children of God. (Romans 8:12–14 NLT)

Disconnected and Connected

There's a situation described in Scripture (Matthew 17:14–21; Mark 9:14–29) that sheds additional light on the importance of fasting. Jesus had sent His disciples out to minister, and for the most part, they had been successful in healing and blessing those they met. But then they encountered a very serious case, a boy possessed by a demon, and they couldn't heal him. The boy's father then went to the source of the disciples' power, Jesus Himself:

> And when they had come to the multitude, a man came to Him, kneeling down to Him and saying, "Lord, have mercy on my son, for he is an epileptic and suffers severely; for he often falls into the fire and often into the water. So I brought him to Your disciples, but they could not cure him."
>
> Then Jesus answered and said, "O faithless and perverse generation, how long shall I be with you? How long shall I bear with you? Bring him here to Me." And Jesus rebuked the demon, and it came out of him; and the child was cured from that very hour.
>
> Then the disciples came to Jesus privately and said, "Why could we not cast it out?"
>
> So Jesus said to them, "Because of your unbelief; for assuredly, I say to you, if you have faith as a mustard seed, you will say to this mountain, 'Move from here to there,' and it will move; and nothing will be impossible for you. However, this kind does not go out except by prayer and fasting." (Matthew 17:14–21 NKJV)

Notice that Jesus identified two problems with the disciples' inability to heal this boy. First, He said they were "faithless"—not connected to God as their singular power source. Faith is built through connection with God, spending time with Him and experiencing Him fully. While their intentions may have been good, the disciples had apparently drifted in their faith.

This was likely caused by the second problem—being too connected to the world. The word translated here as "perverse" literally means corrupted, having too much of the world in us. This is the same kind of worldliness Paul was talking about in 1 Corinthians 3. Keep in mind Jesus said His disciples were too worldly at a time that arguably didn't have nearly as many worldly distractions as ours today.

We don't truly realize just how connected to the world we actually are—and how much that connection corrupts us. Jesus told His disciples that they were disconnected from God and too connected to the world. If you stop and think about your own life for a moment, I suspect you'll realize that we're the same way today.

We're partially connected to God when it's convenient for our schedules and we feel like it—on Sundays and when our small group meets, on those mornings when we feel unrushed and can spend time in prayer the way we prefer. If that sounds harsh, please know I'm talking about myself here too. Everyone struggles with being solely connected to God and disconnected from the world.

But Jesus went on to give His disciples the solution to overcoming these two big problems, and it applies to us just as much today as it did to them then. He revealed to them how to get more connected to Him and how to get more disconnected from the world:

> Then the disciples came to Jesus privately and said, "Why could we not cast it out?" So Jesus said to them, "Because of your unbelief; for assuredly, I say to you, if you have faith as a mustard seed, you will say to this mountain, 'Move from here to there,' and it will move; and nothing will be impossible for you. However, this kind does not go out except by prayer and *fasting.*" (Matthew 17:19–21 NKJV, emphasis added)

Just as He identified their two problems, Jesus provided two solutions: prayer and fasting. Notice how these remedy the problems. First, prayer connects us to God and restores our intimacy and reliance on Him and Him alone. Second, fasting disconnects us from the world and its temptations, distractions, and appeals to our fleshly appetites. It's a discipline in which we push away the things of the flesh.

As Paul described it, and as we've probably all experienced at various times, the issue is our flesh, our carnal selves and their selfish, sinful desires. Fasting requires us to starve our flesh and put it to death. By temporarily denying ourselves, we're awakening our hunger for spiritual things. The goal is not starvation or physical death but a fuller life in which bodily desires are properly ordered beneath spiritual desire for God. We abstain from whatever we usually use to fill our spirits other than God—food, entertainment, news, social media, whatever we rely on for comfort and pleasure.

In the process of suppressing and starving your flesh by fasting, your spirit comes alive and grows stronger. Just as prayer strengthens your connection with God, fasting weakens your body and your soul's worldly desires. Returning to Paul again, we see how he described this same solution that Christ had shared with His disciples:

> Therefore, dear brothers and sisters, you have no obligation to do what your sinful nature urges you to do. For if you live by its dictates, you will die. But if through the power of the Spirit you *put to death* the deeds of your sinful nature, *you will live.* For all who are led by the Spirit of God are children of God. (Romans 8:12–14 NLT, emphasis added)

Starving and Thriving

Fasting is mentioned in the Bible not a couple times, not a dozen times, but more than seventy times! In fact, Jesus said that His people would need to fast to remain connected to Him in His absence, once He had left earth and returned to heaven: "Then John's disciples came and asked him, 'How is it that we and the Pharisees fast often, but your disciples do not *fast*?' Jesus answered, 'How can the guests of the bridegroom mourn while he is with them? The time will come when the bridegroom will be taken from them; *then they will fast*'" (Matthew 9:14–15 NIV, emphasis added).

Fasting was a vital part of life in the New Testament church, in both big decisions and daily moments. "While they were worshiping the Lord and *fasting*, the Holy Spirit said, 'Set apart for me Barnabas and Saul for the work to which I have called them.' So after they had *fasted and prayed*, they placed their hands on them and sent them off" (Acts 13:2–3 NIV, emphasis added). We also find that the apostle Paul fasted as a regular discipline: "... in weariness and toil, in sleeplessness often, in hunger and thirst, in fastings often" (2 Corinthians 11:27 NKJV). I sincerely believe fasting is not an optional habit or an only-if-you-feel-like-it spiritual discipline. It is essential to our spiritual lives.

Fasting is mentioned in the Bible not a couple times, not a dozen times, but more than seventy times!

Keep in mind that fasting encompasses much more than food. I realize that some people are unable to fast from food due to physical conditions or medications they take. In fact, I urge you never to fast without checking with your doctor first and other health professionals you trust. You want to use wisdom when denying yourself fleshly desires, not jeopardize your physical, mental, and emotional health.

If you're unable to fast from food for whatever reason, don't assume that fasting is irrelevant to your faith. There are plenty of other pleasures and distractions that anyone desiring to connect to God can give up—secular music and movies, video games, social media, and basically any pastime used to provide escape, comfort, pleasure, and relief.

Here's what you will discover through fasting if you haven't already:

Whatever you starve *dies*.
Whatever you feed *thrives*.

In the following chapters we'll explore ways you can fast based on the nine different fasts described in the Bible. We'll examine why people fasted in these ways and the results they encountered. I'll share more of my own personal experiences with fasting, along with stories from our church family that have come out of our semiannual 21 Days of Prayer. God always moves so powerfully at Highlands during those three-week seasons of prayer every year in January and August, when we disconnect from the world and refocus on Him.

My hope is that you'll see that fasting isn't something that should intimidate you or make you nervous and that it also isn't something you should ignore or neglect. Fasting is an essential spiritual practice that will strengthen your spirit in a powerful way as you dull your appetites for the things of this world. As you lean into fasting, you will supercharge your prayer life with a stronger, more focused connection with God and a looser attachment to the world.

fourteen

practical keys to fasting

―――――――

I became my own only when I
gave myself to Another.

―C. S. Lewis

Fasting supercharges our prayer lives by eliminating
many if not most of the distractions we usually face. As we
explored in the previous chapter, prayer connects us to God and
fasting disconnects us from the world. Fasting allows us to quiet
the appetites of our bodies and the desires of our souls so our
spirits can grow stronger and closer to God.

Interestingly, as we deny ourselves what we usually use to
fuel our bodies and souls in order to feed our spirits, fasting can

actually benefit our bodies. Medical studies have shown that fasting triggers stem-cell regeneration of our immune system. A study at the University of California in 2014 concluded that cycles of prolonged fasting not only protect against immune system damage but actually "induce immune system regeneration, shifting stem cells from a dormant state to a state of self-renewal."[3]

Such studies provide medical validation for the benefits of fasting and honor the lives of the many Christian leaders and pastors who have taught the power of fasting to ignite one's prayer life. I think of people like Dr. Bill Bright, who cofounded Campus Crusade for Christ, now known as Cru, alongside his wife, Vonette. The Brights were longstanding practitioners of fasting and believed it was one of the most powerful spiritual disciplines.

When Dr. Bright was awarded the Templeton Prize for Progress in Religion in 1996, he invested the one-million-dollar cash prize for the research and development of fasting.[4] The results of his investment continue to reap dividends today in the lives of millions of believers around the world. His example and the legacy of his work contributed some of the most valuable resources in my own exploration and practice of fasting.[5]

Why Fast?

As you consider the role fasting can play in your spiritual life, I encourage you to begin by setting your objective. Consider why you wish to fast and decide what you hope to experience by participating. Choosing your focus can help you decide what kind of fast to do.

> **There are just as many reasons to fast as there are reasons to pray.**

There are just as many reasons to fast as there are reasons to pray. If you're uncertain about what you hope to gain from fasting, reflect on these questions:

1. Are you in need of healing or a miracle?
2. Do you need a fresh encounter with God in your life?
3. Is there a dream inside you that only He can make possible?
4. Do you desire a deeper, more intimate and powerful relationship with the Lord?
5. Are you ready to have heightened sensitivity to the desires of God?
6. Do you need to break away from bondages of sin that have been holding you hostage?
7. Do you have a friend or loved one who needs salvation?
8. Do you desire to know God's will for your life?

As you consider your motive for fasting, remember what we're told in James: "You do not have because you do not ask God. When you ask, you do not receive, because you ask with wrong motives, that you may spend what you get on your pleasures" (James 4:2–3 NIV). Make sure that your intentions for fasting are pure: You want to get close to God. You want His voice to be louder than the world's or even your own voice in your life. There are a few specific things I do daily when I fast to keep my focus on drawing near to God. As I share these, I hope they help you set and maintain your intentions for your fast.

Declare Your Dependence on God

As you disconnect from the world by fasting, you become more reliant on God and His Spirit within you. Our church begins each year with 21 days of prayer and fasting because we want to give God the first of our time and attention at the beginning of a new season. What we put first or do first communicates priority. When you give God your first—first part of your day, of your week, of your year, of your income—you declare your dependence on Him for the rest.

Each morning I start the day by greeting the Lord and spending a few moments in prayer before I get out of bed. Before I leave the house, I spend more time with Him because I know it sets the tone for the rest of my day. When it's payday at our house, or any time we receive income, Tammy and I immediately tithe to God before we pay any bills or spend that money on anything else. We're no longer under Old Testament law, but we want to tithe in order to give God our firstfruits as we acknowledge Him as the source of everything we have.

When you give God the first of your time and your finances, you always see a shift. You walk through your day with greater awareness of His presence. You experience greater peace as you reaffirm your trust in Your Provider.

When you give God your first through prayer and fasting, you set the course for your life. Fasting one day a week sets the direction for each week. Fasting at the beginning of a new month or new year sets the course for the rest of that time period. Fasting redirects your attention to the most important priority in your life: your relationship with God.

Ask for Forgiveness

Fasting facilitates reflection and provides the perfect opportunity for confession and a fresh experience of His grace and forgiveness. The act of fasting reflects repentance—your desire to turn away from the things of the world and redirect your life toward God. Fasting is a time for purifying yourself before God. As you empty yourself of your sinful habits, indulgent appetites, and pleasurable distractions, you discover more of God's presence and make room for more of His goodness in your life.

As you ask for and receive God's forgiveness in your own life, you can also pray for repentance and revival in your church, your neighborhood, your community, your nation, and the world. Fasting draws you closer to God, which allows you to gain clarity and pray for areas of need revealed to you, both individually and globally.

Refocus on the Spiritual

It's so easy to get wrapped up in this life—yet our time here on earth is temporary. We get so busy and consumed by what seems urgent day in and day out—constantly working, resolving family problems, trending on social media, battling uncertainty and anxiety. The mundane and the maddening, the profane and

Fasting is a time for purifying yourself before God. As you empty yourself of your sinful habits, indulgent appetites, and pleasurable distractions, you discover more of God's presence and make room for more of His goodness in your life.

the profound all clamor for our attention, diverting us from our priorities even as time slips away. God's Word reminds us, "Our days on earth are like grass; like wildflowers, we bloom and die" (Psalm 103:15 NLT).

In Ecclesiastes, which most Bible scholars believe to be written by the incomparably wise King Solomon, the narrator declares, "Life is fleeting, like a passing mist. It is like trying to catch hold of a breath; all vanishes like a vapor; everything is a great vanity" (Ecclesiastes 1:2 THE VOICE). All the more reason to invest our time, energy, and resources wisely into a legacy with an eternal impact. We can pray the words of the psalmist, "So teach us to number our days that we may get a heart of wisdom" (Psalm 90:12 ESV).

Invite the Presence of God into Your Life

As we give up the pleasures, indulgences, and distractions we've grown accustomed to filling our lives with, fasting makes room in our spirits for God to fill us completely. When I fast, I pray for a divine visitation and more comprehensive sense of God's presence in my life. I like redirecting my attention back to my first love, my relationship with the Lord. I want every part of my life to be filled with His presence, His peace, His wisdom, and His love.

Believe God for Answers to Specific Needs

When you're seeking answers, solutions, direction, and guidance, I can't think of a better way to determine God's direction than by fasting. I suspect many times when we pray our requests, God answers us but we simply can't hear the whisper of His Spirit in our lives amid the clamor of the world. In the technology-driven twenty-first century, we've grown accustomed to multitasking—texting, reading, watching TV, listening to music, playing video games, often at the same time.

Fasting is a time to remove all the noise and still ourselves before God so that we can hear His voice in our lives. Jesus said, "My sheep listen to my voice; I know them, and they follow me" (John 10:27 NIV). When you fast, your senses—certainly in your spirit—grow more acute. What are you believing God for? What questions do you have that only He can answer?

Fasting provides an intimate environment for you to listen and hear your Shepherd's voice.

Four Types of Fasts

Once you've decided to fast, then you must decide what type of fast you will do. Don't feel any pressure to do what others are doing—your fast is solely between you and the Lord. Jesus emphasized the intimacy of your personal choice to fast to His followers:

> "When you fast, do not look somber as the hypocrites do, for they disfigure their faces to show others they are fasting. Truly I tell you, they have received their reward in full. But when you fast, put oil on your head and wash your face, so that it will not be obvious to others that you are fasting, but only to your Father, who is unseen; and your Father, who sees what is done in secret, will reward you." (Matthew 6:16–18 NIV)

As you consider the type of fast you will do, think about the four general types described in Scripture.

Complete Fast

First, and likely most familiar to you, is a *complete fast* from all solid foods. This fast calls for drinking only liquids, typically water with light juices occasionally. You stay hydrated and nourish yourself without chewing. Once again, always seek medical supervision and the approval of your doctor and health-care professionals before beginning any kind of fast that involves your diet and nutrition.

If I may be blunt, just use common sense. Don't attempt to fast if you have medical or dietary reasons that prohibit you from abstaining from food. The goal is not to lose weight or even to experience the health benefits that accompany fasting. The goal is to experience the "spirit of fasting," which can only happen in your spirit.

Selective Fast

The second type of fast to consider is a selective fast. This kind of fasting involves removing certain elements from your diet. Perhaps the best example of this is often called the Daniel Fast. After being taken captive by the Babylonians, Daniel "resolved not to defile himself with the royal food and wine" and instead asked the king's attendant, "Please test your servants for ten days: Give us nothing but vegetables to eat and water to drink" (Daniel 1:8, 12 NIV). Later in his captivity, we're told Daniel mourned for three weeks: "I ate no choice food; no meat or wine touched my

lips; and I used no lotions at all until the three weeks were over"
(Daniel 10:3 NIV).

If you decide to follow Daniel's example, you remove everything from your diet except vegetables and water. Other selective
fasts remove sugar, dairy, or grains—similar to the Whole30
program. Once again, the goal is to simplify and purify your
diet and focus instead on your relationship with God.

Partial Fast

This fast is sometimes called the Jewish Fast because it
involves foregoing certain meals, just as Jewish people tradition-
ally did and still do for certain observances. For a partial fast, you
might decide to fast all day and only eat one meal in the evening.
Or you eat only one meal each day, using the other mealtimes for
prayer and other spiritual practices, such as Bible study or praying
communally.

This type has grown in popularity due to the trend of
intermittent fasting, which is a partial fast chosen for health
reasons—to lose weight or lower cholesterol. While health benefits are great, they should not be what motivates you. Seeking
a deeper connection with God is the spiritual motive for your
fasting experience.

Soul Fast

The fourth type of fast deprives your soul of the comforts,
pleasures, and preoccupations that usually fill your time and
attention. Anything that fits this description can be put aside
for your fast—social media, movies, news, TV shows, secular

music, video games, pet videos on TikTok, whatever it might be. The goal is to move away from life as usual and your default methods of zoning out and move toward God by using that time for prayer and Bible reading.

Remember, fasting is a matter of your heart, not your diet. It's not about food as much as it's about removing things from your life so you can draw close to God. Sometimes the fast itself can become a distraction, especially if you're new to this practice. Fasting is not about gritting yourself through a discipline to say you accomplished it. Fasting is about surrendering your appetites to God to feast on more of Him.

With this goal in mind, do whatever you can to prepare yourself. Even before you begin your fast, repent of any sin in your life and prepare your heart for realigning with the Lord. Put aside anything that grieves the Holy Spirit. As you may have heard before, it's time to "get right with God." God's Word repeatedly makes this command clear: "'Even now,' declares the LORD, 'return to me with all your heart, with fasting and weeping and mourning.' Rend your heart and not your garments. Return to the LORD your God.'" (Joel 2:12–13 NIV).

Great Expectations

Regardless of the type of fast you choose, expect results. For inspiration, consider what's often called the "fasting chapter" in the Bible, Isaiah 58. There, you can catch a glimpse of what to expect during your fasting experience: "Then your light will break forth like the dawn, and your *healing* will quickly appear; then your *righteousness* will go before you, and the glory of the LORD will be your rear guard. Then you will call, and the LORD will *answer*; you will cry for help, and he will say: Here am I" (Isaiah 58:8–9 NIV, emphasis added).

Your expectations should include *healing*. If some area of your life is broken or not right, if something needs to be healed, then God can mend those broken pieces as you draw close to Him. This includes physical and mental healing. If you suffer from depression and anxiety, expect God's peace to mend your heart and illuminate your darkness.

You should also expect to encounter more of God's *holiness* and *righteousness*. Habits, thoughts, relationships, and situations may not be perfect—nothing in this fallen world can be completely perfect this side of heaven—but things can be restored and set on the right course again. Remember, holiness means being set apart by God for His purposes. When you experience His righteousness and recognize He has set you apart, you realign with your holy purpose.

Finally, expect to receive God's *help*. Disconnecting from the world by fasting enables you to receive God's favor and blessing in your life. You gain clarity and focus, allowing you to see your life and relationships from His point of view—which in turn enables you to resolve conflicts, overcome obstacles, and remedy problems that once seemed insurmountable.

Expect to be surprised, spiritually energized, and filled with the fresh air of God's Spirit!

Breaking Your Fast

Regardless of the type of fast you undertake, it's important to take caution when you break the fast. You will want to be careful, both physically and spiritually, when breaking a fast because you have changed, both inside and out. Physically, you want to be careful reintroducing certain types of foods into your body because you've adapted to going without them. Meat, sweets, and rich foods may be harmful when overloaded into your system after any kind of dietary fast.

Spiritually, you want to be careful not to let down your guard as you end your fast. The devil is always looking for an opportune time. While your spirit may be stronger than ever, your body and soul may be at their weakest points. Remember that the Enemy chose to tempt Jesus immediately after He had been praying and fasting in the wilderness.

I also encourage you to end your fast gradually rather than abruptly. Give yourself time to reacclimate to your previous lifestyle habits and diet. I have seen too many people experience a big setback immediately after a successful fast. They go back to their old way of living and rush into what had been distracting, tempting, and harming them before their fast. In fact, some things that we eliminate during our fasts should never return. Jesus explained:

> "When an impure spirit comes out of a person, it goes through
> arid places seeking rest and does not find it. Then it says, 'I will

return to the house I left.' When it arrives, it finds the house swept clean and put in order. Then it goes and takes seven other spirits more wicked than itself, and they go in and live there. And the final condition of that person is worse than the first." (Luke 11:24–26 NIV)

In other words, when depriving your body and soul of what they crave, you might experience a boomerang effect when they come rushing back with ravenous appetites. You don't want to lose the closeness to God that you've just experienced before it can permeate all areas of your life.

Fasting disconnects you from worldly things so you can connect to that which is eternal.

Fasting is not a spiritual cure-all or one-time experience. We need fresh encounters with the Holy Spirit every day. To keep our spirits strong and connected to God more than the world, we also need new times of fasting throughout the year. Remember, fasting disconnects you from worldly things so you can connect to that which is eternal.

fifteen

nine fasts in the Bible

———

So we fasted and petitioned our God
about this, and he answered our prayer.

—Ezra 8:23 NIV

Newcomers at our church are often surprised that not
only do we encourage fasting as a spiritual practice but we also
join together to fast corporately each year. We remind them that
in both the Old Testament and the New Testament, fasting was
a common practice. Followers of Jesus in the early church fasted
as a regular part of their prayer and worship habits. Only in the
past one hundred years or so has fasting seemed to decline in
practice within the lifestyle of most churches. But Jesus told

His followers, "*When* you fast," not *if* you fast (Matthew 6:16 NIV, emphasis added).

Consequently, many people find it helpful to see how fasting was practiced by various people in the Bible. Based on their examples, fasting usually serves as a conduit for praying—often during intense times of preparation, loss, uncertainty, and celebration. Fasting is mentioned more than seventy times in the Bible, and while we can categorize them in various ways, I count nine reasons or motivations fasts are used to accompany prayer. Let's briefly consider each one and how it applies to our prayer lives today.

1. To Prepare for Ministry

After His baptism but before He began His public ministry on earth, Jesus spent forty days and nights fasting and praying in the wilderness (Matthew 4:1–17; Mark 1:12–13; Luke 4:1–14). As I mentioned in chapter 11, Christ also experienced temptations from the Enemy during this time of preparation. The devil likely hoped to stop Jesus' public ministry before it even started. If the Evil One could cause God's Son to sin while in human form, then perhaps Christ's power would be diminished while on earth and His ministry rendered ineffective.

I suspect the Enemy targets us even more deliberately when we're about to begin a new ministry, outreach, group, service, or any kind of event or initiative where God will be honored and glorified. You'll recall my daughter's health crisis with her eye the same week our newly formed church launched its first big public outreach.

I don't dread or fear the Enemy's assaults, but I do prepare for whatever we're doing with more care, attention to detail, and determination. I know that the only way to endure demonic attacks with patience, stamina, and faith is by relying entirely on God. Fasting helps me do that. It keeps me humble and restores my focus on the big picture, the eternal perspective from God's point of view.

Fasting also prepares me for ministry by reminding me of my limits. In other words, whatever is about to happen isn't up to me. I recall Moses heading up Mount Sinai to receive the Ten Commandments: "When I went up on the mountain to receive the tablets of stone, the tablets of the covenant that the LORD had made with you, I stayed on the mountain forty days and forty nights; I ate no bread and drank no water" (Deuteronomy 9:9 NIV).

The deep, abiding connection I experience with God when fasting and praying sustains me when I'm stepping out of my comfort zone or facing obstacles seemingly impossible to overcome. Any big initiative or new ministry our church launches is always preceded by prayer and fasting by as many intercessors as possible. Fasting and praying lay the foundation for God to use you to accomplish more than you could ever do on your own.

2. To Seek God's Wisdom

When you're making important decisions, it's always a good idea to seek God's wisdom and allow His Spirit to guide you.

When your decisions impact others and require you to assess the leadership abilities of others, then you want to be totally reliant on God. We see this kind of fasting when members of the early church made crucial decisions. For example, as they traveled and evangelized throughout Lystra, Iconium, and Antioch, "Paul and Barnabas appointed elders for them in each church and, with prayer and fasting, committed them to the Lord, in whom they had put their trust" (Acts 14:23 NIV).

When you don't know what to do—and even when you think you do—it's always a good idea to pray first. If the weight of your decision carries greater consequences, for you and others, then you want the Spirit to lead you. Fasting can remove the noise and clamor of other voices vying for your attention, which will allow you to hear God clearly and move forward confidently.

> Fasting can remove the noise and clamor of other voices vying for your attention, which will allow you to hear God clearly and move forward confidently.

Every time I make a big decision, particularly one that impacts my family, my team, and our church, prayer is essential. If I feel that I need confirmation or still harbor some uncertainty, then fasting clears the spiritual airwaves so that I can hear the Holy Spirit. God's Word provides wisdom, commands, and guidelines for our lives. But how we apply them in the context of various situations, events, and relationships often requires supernatural wisdom and discernment. Fasting can help facilitate this.

3. To Seek God's Power for Protection

Whenever travel and logistics are involved, the only certainty I trust is prayer for whatever happens unexpectedly. Prayer keeps me calm when flights are delayed, connections are missed, and events are canceled at the last minute. Depending on the scope and magnitude and what I sense in my spirit, I often fast and pray to ask for God's protection and traveling mercies. It might be when I'm driving to an event or when my kids and their families are going overseas. Often I pray for God's power and protection when our church is hosting events in which hundreds or thousands of people will be traveling to us.

In the Bible we see this kind of prayer and fasting when the people of Israel finally left captivity in Babylon to return home. Facing a trek of more than nine hundred miles back to Jerusalem, Ezra declared a time of communal fasting to pray and ask God for safe travels:

> There, by the Ahava Canal, I proclaimed a fast, so that we might humble ourselves before our God and ask him for a safe journey for us and our children, with all our possessions. I was ashamed to ask the king for soldiers and horsemen to protect us from enemies on the road, because we had told the king, "The gracious hand of our God is on everyone who looks to him, but his great anger is against all who forsake him." So we fasted and petitioned our God about this, and he answered our prayer. (Ezra 8:21–23 NIV)

4. To Express Grief and to Mourn

When the Jewish exiles left Babylon and finally reached Israel, they found their homeland in ruins. Led by Ezra and Nehemiah, they began rebuilding the city wall around Jerusalem. By this time the people of Israel had forgotten God's law and the scriptures, but Ezra found scrolls containing God's Word, which he began reading to the Israelites. Shamed by their awareness of how far they had strayed from God, the people tore their robes and wept. Ezra then proclaimed a fast in order to pray and mourn.

> I questioned them about the Jewish remnant that had survived the exile, and also about Jerusalem. They said to me, "Those who survived the exile and are back in the province are in great trouble and disgrace. The wall of Jerusalem is broken down, and its gates have been burned with fire."
>
> When I heard these things, I sat down and wept. For some days I mourned and fasted and prayed before the God of heaven. (Nehemiah 1:2–4 NIV)

Fasting and praying also occurred when people mourned the loss of individual lives. After David interrogated an outsider with news of the king's death, he and his army were overcome with the magnitude of the loss. David's grief must have been compounded by the loss of his beloved soul-friend Jonathan, the king's son. We're told, "They mourned and wept and fasted till evening for Saul and his son Jonathan, and for the army of the LORD and for the nation of Israel, because they had fallen by the sword" (2 Samuel 1:12 NIV).

Anytime we experience significant loss, we grieve and look for a way forward in the midst of sadness, anger, and sorrow. When we feel overwhelmed, we often turn to God for comfort and His peace that passes human understanding. Fasting intensifies our connection to Him and allows us to experience His presence and peace more powerfully.

5. To Repent and Return to God

Fasting is also an appropriate response when mourning our sinful disobedience and humbling ourselves before God. Fasting and praying reflect that we are acutely aware of our sin and how we've turned away from God, while also indicating our desire to be forgiven and return to Him. We pull away from the temptations, distractions, and worldly influences that may have contributed to our decision to stray and restore our focus to our relationship with God.

We find a powerful example of this kind of prayer and fasting after God sent Jonah to Nineveh to pronounce judgment and condemnation. Distraught and desperate, the king dressed in sackcloth and sat in ashes and then commanded people to fast and pray. Their corporate repentance moved God to show His mercy: "When God saw what they did and how they turned from their evil ways, he relented and did not bring on them the destruction he had threatened" (Jonah 3:10 NIV).

We also see a similar catalyst for prayer and fasting once again in the life of Moses. You'll recall that he fasted and prayed for forty days and nights in preparation for receiving the Ten Commandments. But things didn't exactly go as he expected because while Moses was on the mountain receiving God's commandments, the people of Israel rebelled against the Lord in dramatic fashion—by creating a golden calf to idolize.

When Moses learned of their brazen disobedience, he angrily shattered the stone tablets upon which the commandments were written. Which meant he had to go back and get a new set—but not before he fasted and prayed on behalf of the Jewish people: "Then once again I fell prostrate before the LORD for forty days and forty nights; I ate no bread and drank no water, because of all the sin you had committed, doing what was evil in the LORD's sight and so arousing his anger" (Deuteronomy 9:18 NIV).

6. To Seek God's Power for Victory

Fasting intensifies our prayerful requests, which is often required when fighting a battle. Once again, we begin to see the ways these reasons and motives for fasting can overlap, preparing one to hear what God has to say and receive what He wants to give.

While fighting the Benjamites, the other tribes of Israel lost forty thousand men in the first two days of battle. Consequently, the whole army went to Bethel, the location of the ark of the covenant, and "sat weeping before the LORD," crying out for His help to overcome their enemy (Judges 20:26 NIV). "They fasted that day until evening and presented burnt offerings and fellowship offerings to the LORD" (Judges 20:26 NIV).

When they asked God if they should resume battle, He replied, "Go, for tomorrow I will give them into your hands" (Judges 20:28 NIV). Obeying God's instruction, the Israelites resumed the fierce battle, resulting in thousands of additional casualties, before ultimately conquering the Benjamites (Judges 20:30–36).

> When we face overwhelming odds for defeat or face an intimidating adversary, fasting and praying for God's power is often required for victory.

While our battles may not be military campaigns, when we face overwhelming odds for defeat or face an intimidating adversary, fasting and praying for God's power is often required for victory.

7. To Worship God

Some of the most powerful, all-consuming times of praise and worship I've ever experienced occurred during our 21 Days of Prayer. Without so many other sights, sounds, and demands pulling at us, we're free to focus singularly on the Lord, on who He is. His goodness, power, mercy, and love are so overwhelming, there's no fitting response except to worship Him for who He is.

During these times of sweet communion with God, I've

often thought of an eighty-four-year-old woman mentioned only briefly in the Bible. When Mary and Joseph brought young Jesus to the temple in Jerusalem to be consecrated according to the law of Moses, they encountered an elderly prophet named Anna, who "never left the temple but worshiped night and day, fasting and praying" (Luke 2:37 NIV). Apparently, Anna's prayers were answered because she lived to see the Messiah: "Coming up to them at that very moment, she gave thanks to God and spoke about the child to all who were looking forward to the redemption of Jerusalem" (Luke 2:38 NIV).

Fasting shows our devotion to God as we make Him our only priority and preoccupation. There are no richer, more powerful times of worshiping God than when we fast and pray.

8. To Seek God's Favor in Desperate Situations

Desperate times call for desperate measures—and fasting may be the best desperate measure of all. As you know by now, prayer should be our first response and not our last resort. But sometimes when prayer alone doesn't seem to be enough, or when we haven't been able to receive God's answer to our prayers, fasting can provide the extra push we need to draw closer to God. In situations when we're called to do the overwhelming, improbable, or outright impossible, fasting and praying increases our connection to God, which in turn strengthens our spirits, clears our minds, and inspires our hearts.

When the Israelites were exiled in Babylon, the king chose a young Hebrew woman named Esther to be his queen. Living in the Babylonian palace, Esther learned that Haman, one of the king's officials, planned to kill all the Jews. Esther struggled with what she could do to prevent the annihilation of her people. While she had access to the king and could explain Haman's plot, she also knew that anyone who initiated a conversation with the king, rather than waiting to be asked to speak, could face capital punishment.

Deciding to take the only course of action available, even at her own peril, Esther first fasted and asked those in her community to fast with her: "Go, gather together all the Jews who are in Susa, and fast for me. Do not eat or drink for three days, night or day. I and my attendants will fast as you do. When this is done, I will go to the king, even though it is against the law. And if I perish, I perish" (Esther 4:16 NIV).

Esther's courage was bolstered by fasting and praying individually as well as corporately. When you are at the end of your rope or don't see a way forward, asking others to join you as you fast and pray is one of the most powerful ways they can help you.

9. To Engage in Spiritual Warfare

Because we've already explored warfare prayers, I won't repeat what we covered in chapter 11. I will, however, remind you that Jesus Himself indicated that our faith is empowered by fasting, which is apparently what's required when facing the Enemy and his demons (Mark 9:29). You certainly don't have to wait until confronted by "this kind" of demon in your life; you can take preventive measures by making fasting a part of your regular prayer life. But when nothing else seems to work, think of fasting as the spiritual advantage you may need to add.

When you're engaging in spiritual warfare, the devil will use anything he can to disrupt, distract, and divert you from serving God. Fasting supercharges your prayers so that you access more of the Holy Spirit's power and overcome anything the devil throws at you. Notice how Paul instructed us before he listed the spiritual armor we're to use in warfare:

> Finally, be strong in the Lord and in his mighty power. Put on the full armor of God, so that you can take your stand against the devil's schemes. For our struggle is not against flesh and blood, but against the rulers, against the authorities, against the powers of this dark world and against the spiritual forces of evil in the heavenly realms.

Then, immediately after completing his description of each piece of armor, Paul urged:

> And pray in the Spirit on all occasions with all kinds of prayers and requests. With this in mind, be alert and always keep on praying for all the Lord's people. Pray also for me, that whenever I speak, words may be given me so that I will fearlessly make known the mystery of the gospel, for which I am an

ambassador in chains. Pray that I may declare it fearlessly, as I should. (Ephesians 6:10–12, 18–20 NIV)

Notice that he instructed us to pray on *all occasions* in *all the ways* we know how to pray. We're not only to pray for ourselves but for "*all* the Lord's people." He then asked the recipients of his letter to pray for him, that he may continue proclaiming the gospel "fearlessly." And he asked more than once, repeating his desire to overcome any fears he might be facing.

Fasting intensifies your prayers so that you can cover yourself as well as those around you with spiritual armor against the Enemy's assaults and deceptions.

Fast Forward

Fasting must never become a practice that leaves us feeling entitled to receive our requests. Remember, fasting is not about food but about your heart. The people of Israel practiced fasting even while openly rebelling and disobeying God. They didn't understand why their prayers were not answered even though they fasted:

> "Why have we fasted," they say,
> "and you have not seen it?
> Why have we humbled ourselves,
> and you have not noticed?"

> Yet on the day of your fasting, you do as you please
>> and exploit all your workers.
> Your fasting ends in quarreling and strife,
>> and in striking each other with wicked fists.
> You cannot fast as you do today
>> and expect your voice to be heard on high.
>
> (Isaiah 58:3-4 NIV)

Notice that all nine of these reasons and motives for fasting have one thing in common: a desire to depend solely on God. There's nothing magic or spiritually powerful in the act of fasting by itself. Fasting simply clears everything else away so that you can channel all aspects of yourself solely on God. Fasting can move you forward in your relationship with God.

Like so many other believers who fast regularly, I'm convinced fasting is a powerful tool used by the Holy Spirit to strengthen our faith and transform us in the image of Jesus. As a spiritual practice, fasting unplugs us from the busyness of the world that typically consumes our time, energy, and attention and allows us to engage more fully with God at a deep, intimate level. Fasting allows us to listen to God's Spirit as it reveals our spiritual condition, spotlights sin, and urges us to repent and receive God's grace and mercy.

Based on my own experience and that shared by others, fasting helps us retain and absorb God's Word more fully and effectively. Without so many other worldly distractions, we can meditate on His Word and allow it to permeate our hearts and

There's nothing magic or spiritually powerful in the act of fasting by itself. Fasting simply clears everything else away so that you can channel all aspects of yourself solely on God.

minds. The Bible has never seemed more alive to me than when I'm fasting and focused on knowing God at a deeper level.

Fasting allows your relationship with God to be even more personal and uniquely your own. You fall in love with Him again and again as you recognize who He is and all He has done for you. As you experience a greater awareness of how much God loves you, your faith becomes bolder. You trust God and become more willing to take risks and step out in faith.

And you want others to know God at this same, intimate level. When you experience spiritual revival and rejuvenation through fasting, you become a conduit of God's love, grace, and hope to others. You become more passionate and active about sharing your faith with others in every way possible. They see what a difference your intimacy with God makes, and it taps into their own longing to know more of Him.

Simply put, fasting allows you to draw closer to God than you would otherwise.

So pray first—and fast regularly!

sixteen

21 days of prayer and fasting

———

Our seasons of fasting and prayer at the
Tabernacle have been high days indeed; never
has heaven's gate stood wider; never have
our hearts been nearer the central glory.

—Charles Spurgeon

Three weeks is a long time, and thinking about it in terms
of 21 days seems even longer. But in light of eternity, I can't think
of any better way to boost your faith than with this concentrated
amount of time. I've been starting each new year with 21 days of

prayer and fasting since the 1990s. I chose 21 days based on the Daniel Fast.

While in captivity in Babylon, a place known for its extravagant indulgences, Daniel not only kept his faith in God—he actually used his seventy years there to influence the Babylonian culture. When the king insisted that Daniel and a select group of young Israelites eat lavish meals and drink royal wine from the king's table, Daniel refused and maintained a diet of vegetables, grains, and water (Daniel 1:8–16). Later, after receiving a disturbing vision of an imminent war, Daniel chose to restrict his diet once again: "I ate no choice food; no meat or wine touched my lips; and I used no lotions at all until the three weeks were over" (Daniel 10:3 NIV).

All to say, if it was good enough for Daniel, I assumed it was more than good enough for me. When I began starting each year with 21 days of prayer and fasting, I was a young associate pastor on staff at a church in Louisiana. After being called by God to serve, I focused on studying the Bible, learning from mentors and other pastors, and serving others as the Spirit led. During this time I was also starting a family with my bride, Tammy. We were both sold out to God and wanted to do whatever He asked, wherever He led.

As I gained pastoral experience, though, I began to feel unsettled—not about serving God but about my current status. It wasn't that I longed to move to another state and start a new church from scratch, but I sensed God was preparing me for something beyond anything I could imagine. Finally, I reached a place where I began feeling stuck—emotionally and spiritually. I battled anxiety and experienced depression but didn't know how to break free and move forward.

It was time for something new.

God's Vision

Already committed to the power of prayer to strengthen my connection to God, I felt called to fast. January, right after the busyness of Christmas and the holiday season, seemed like a good time to hold this time of prayer and fasting. Instead of New Year's resolutions, I wanted to give God all my time and attention right off the bat, making it clear that my relationship with Him is my first priority.

My excitement and enthusiasm, along with a lot of powerful praise and worship, saw me through that first week. But then it started getting more difficult. My body wasn't used to being deprived of solid food. My soul wasn't used to giving up control over what I ate and how I spent my time each day. But that was the point—I needed a change, a breakthrough, to show me a new way forward.

And that's exactly what God gave me. When I had the vision during the 21 days of prayer and fasting in 2000, I saw myself preaching on a stage before hundreds if not thousands of people, but I didn't know what city it was in. So after the fast, in May of 2000, Tammy and I loaded up our kids and took our vacation time to travel around to various cities in hopes of finding out where God was leading me.

Birmingham, Alabama, was on the list because I had attended the Southeastern Conference (SEC) college baseball tournament there the previous three years, and I was falling in love with the city. So along with the other seven cities we were considering, I took the entire family to Birmingham during the SEC baseball tournament.

One morning on the way to the ballpark, I stopped at the Starbucks in a Barnes & Noble bookstore that overlooked the busiest road in Alabama, Highway 280. Outside the bookshop with my coffee in hand, I looked over the six lanes of traffic and heard God say in my spirit, *You're going to pastor the people in that traffic jam.* Immediately, I knew God was calling me to Birmingham. And that was the day I decided to move my family to that city to start Church of the Highlands in 2001.

As details began to fall into place, I knew without a doubt that prayer and fasting would remain integral to the health and impact of this new church. So when we launched Church of the Highlands, we started it the same way God had revealed it to me— with 21 days of prayer and fasting. Six years later we completed our first building, in an area known as Grants Mill, and built it exactly to match the vision I saw during that first life-changing 21 days of prayer and fasting.

As I said, 21 days is a loooong time when you're going without things you're used to having. While many distractions are eliminated, the tendency to lose focus remains. The Enemy doesn't want you drawing closer to God and growing stronger in His Spirit, so he will try to tempt you with extra-appealing versions of whatever you've given up.

For example, I never receive as many enticing invitations to travel and speak as I do for the month of January. And as hard as it is sometimes to turn them down, it's easy in the sense that my decision has already been made. God gets the first of each new year. I don't have to think about it or deliberate. It's a commitment I intend to keep for the rest of my life.

Knowing temptations will come our way and that it's easy to lose our spiritual focus, I try to help by giving people in our church a daily focus, which I will now share with you. You can use these as you go through your own 21 days in January, or to join together in fasting with your church community, or use them throughout the year, one day at a time. Of course, you can also pray through all 21 focus points in a single day.

There's nothing prescriptive here—I'm only trying to help you focus. Most people tell me that other than a handful of things—family, health, relationships, finances—they're not sure what to pray for. So this 21-day guide shows you some ways to expand your prayer vision and advance God's kingdom through this special time of intimacy with Him. As you're about to see, there's plenty to consider.

Focus for Every Day

Before we get to the 21 points of focus, I want to include a half dozen things I recommend you do every single day of your fast:

1. **Humble yourself.** As you pray, ask for forgiveness for your own sins as well as the sins of your land. Call on

God's promise in His Word: "If my people, who are called by my name, will humble themselves and pray and seek my face and turn from their wicked ways, then I will hear from heaven, and I will forgive their sin and will heal their land" (2 Chronicles 7:14 NIV).

2. **Seek God.** Declare your dependence on God in every area of your life. Renounce anything you may have been relying on other than Him. Obey the instruction in Scripture: "Look to the LORD and his strength; seek his face always" (1 Chronicles 16:11 NIV).

3. **Pray that His kingdom come.** Pray for the completion of the Great Commission and for revival in our generation. Ask the Lord to use you to reflect His love for others so that they might know Him as you partner with Him to advance His kingdom purposes here: "Your kingdom come, your will be done, on earth as it is in heaven" (Matthew 6:10 NIV).

4. **Ask to hear from heaven.** Invite the presence of God into your life, your church, your community, your city, and your nation. Pray for signs, wonders, and miracles so that souls may be saved and lives transformed: "If your Presence does not go with us, do not send us up from here" (Exodus 33:15 NIV).

5. **Believe God for answered prayer to your specific needs.** Surrender your needs to God, and trust Him to take care of you. "Do not be anxious about anything, but in every situation, by prayer and petition, with thanksgiving, present your requests to God" (Philippians 4:6 NIV).

6. **Pray for others.** Ask God to empower those you're praying for to take their next steps in their journeys of faith to know God, find freedom, discover purpose, and make a difference. "I keep asking that the God of our Lord Jesus Christ, the glorious Father, may give you the Spirit of wisdom and revelation, so that you may know him better. I pray that the eyes of your heart may be enlightened in order that you may know the hope to which he has called you, the riches of his glorious inheritance in his holy people" (Ephesians 1:17–18 NIV).

21 Days of Prayer

Committing to prayer and fasting for 21 days allows your relationship with God to go to a deeper level. When you pray corporately with other believers for three weeks, you also enjoy a special bonding experience as you draw closer to God together. You experience a deeper connection to the Lord as well as to your brothers and sisters in Christ.

As you can see here, I like to have a larger, weekly focus for each of the three weeks, with each group of seven days supporting its particular week's overarching theme. These can be mixed and matched according to your needs and how the Spirit leads you. But when you're praying and fasting with others during the 21 days, it helps if everyone follows the same order. These are simply intended to provide a sharper, more specific focus for each day on your 21-day adventure of faith.

——————— WEEK 1: ALL ABOUT JESUS ———————

Sunday's Focus: The Lord's Day
Attend church, rest, and reflect.

"Remember the Sabbath day by keeping it holy." (Exodus 20:8 NIV)

Monday's Focus: Dependence on Him
Seek and rely on God's Spirit.

"Not by might nor by power, but by my Spirit," says the LORD Almighty. (Zechariah 4:6 NIV)

Tuesday's Focus: Surrender to Him
Surrender all areas of your life to God so that you may draw closer to Him and be conformed to the image of Christ.

Therefore, I urge you, brothers and sisters, in view of God's mercy, to offer your bodies as a living sacrifice, holy and pleasing to God—this is your true and proper worship. (Romans 12:1 NIV)

Wednesday's Focus: Worshiping Him
Worship the Lord for who He is and the magnificence of His character.

"Yet a time is coming and has now come when
the true worshipers will worship the Father in the
Spirit and in truth, for they are the kind of worshipers the Father seeks." (John 4:23 NIV)

Thursday's Focus: Broken Before Him
*Confess your sin and experience God's grace and mercy
as you receive His forgiveness.*

My sacrifice, O God, is a broken spirit;
a broken and contrite heart
you, God, will not despise.
(Psalm 51:17 NIV)

Friday's Focus: Listening to Him
*Still yourself before God so that you can hear the voice of
His Spirit.*

"When he has brought out all his own, he goes
on ahead of them, and his sheep follow him
because they know his voice." (John 10:4 NIV)

Saturday's Focus: Casting Your Cares on Him
Place your trust in God and commit yourself to His care.

Commit everything you do to the LORD.
Trust him, and he will help you.
(Psalm 37:5 NLT)

——————— WEEK 2: GOD'S WORK IN ME ———————

Sunday's Focus: The Lord's Day
Attend church, rest, and reflect.

Remember the Sabbath day by keeping it holy. (Exodus 20:8 NIV)

Monday's Focus: My Freedom
Thank God for the freedom you have in Christ.

It is for freedom that Christ has set us free. Stand
firm, then, and do not let yourselves be burdened
again by a yoke of slavery. (Galatians 5:1 NIV)

Tuesday's Focus: My Relationships
*Pray for the important people in your life—immediate
family, loved ones, and close friends.*

Remember the Lord, who is great and awesome, and
fight for your families, your sons and your daughters,
your wives and your homes. (Nehemiah 4:14 NIV)

Wednesday's Focus: My Growth
Ask God to help you grow and mature in your faith.

Speaking the truth in love, we will grow to become
in every respect the mature body of him who is
the head, that is, Christ. (Ephesians 4:15 NIV)

Thursday's Focus: My Calling

Thank the Lord for the calling He has placed on your life to serve Him with your unique abilities and gifts.

But you are a chosen people, a royal priesthood, a holy nation, God's special possession, that you may declare the praises of him who called you out of darkness into his wonderful light. (1 Peter 2:9 NIV)

Friday's Focus: My Healing

Praise God for the ways He has healed you in the past and continues to heal areas of brokenness that need His touch.

"He himself bore our sins" in his body on the cross, so that we might die to sins and live for righteousness; "by his wounds you have been healed." (1 Peter 2:24 NIV)

Saturday's Focus: My Blessing

Give thanks to God for the abundance of blessings in your life right now.

Praise be to the God and Father of our Lord Jesus Christ, who has blessed us in the heavenly realms with every spiritual blessing in Christ. (Ephesians 1:3 NIV)

———————— WEEK 3: INTERCESSION ————————

Sunday's Focus: The Lord's Day
Attend church, rest, and reflect.

> Remember the Sabbath day by keep-
> ing it holy. (Exodus 20:8 NIV)

Monday's Focus: Our Leaders
Lift up in prayer all those in authority over you, including parents, teachers, pastors, local government officials, state leaders, and national leaders, even if you disagree with their ideologies.

> I urge, then, first of all, that petitions, prayers,
> intercession and thanksgiving be made for all
> people—for kings and all those in authority, that
> we may live peaceful and quiet lives in all god-
> liness and holiness. (1 Timothy 2:1–2 NIV)

Tuesday's Focus: Our Missions
Pray for those serving as missionaries and evangelists at all levels—local, national, and international. Lift up specific individuals you know who are committed to spreading the gospel of Jesus Christ to those who do not know Him.

> "But you will receive power when the Holy Spirit
> comes on you; and you will be my witnesses in

Jerusalem, and in all Judea and Samaria, and
to the ends of the earth." (Acts 1:8 NIV)

Wednesday's Focus: Our Church

Ask God to bless, sanctify, and empower His bride, the church, so that it may be salt and light to the dark world. Pray for your pastor and church leaders as well as specific ministries you feel led to lift up.

"And I tell you that you are Peter, and on this rock
I will build my church, and the gates of Hades
will not overcome it." (Matthew 16:18 NIV)

Thursday's Focus: Our Children

Pray for the children in your own family as well as other children you know—in your neighborhood, school, church, and community.

Children are a heritage from the LORD,
offspring a reward from him.
(Psalm 127:3 NIV)

Friday's Focus: The Lost

Pray for all those who do not know God as their Lord and Savior, that they may come to know His love and invite Jesus Christ into their lives. Lift up specific people by name whom you know need the Lord.

The Lord is not slow in keeping his promise, as
some understand slowness. Instead he is patient
with you, not wanting anyone to perish, but
everyone to come to repentance. (2 Peter 3:9 NIV)

Saturday's Focus: Our Victory

*Give God thanks and praise for all the incredible things
He has shown you over the past 21 days.*

But thanks be to God! He gives us the victory through
our Lord Jesus Christ. (1 Corinthians 15:57 NIV)

Don't be surprised when your prayer experience grows
richer with each passing day, each consecutive week.
Praying and fasting for 21 days is truly a spiritual adventure unlike any other. Your commitment to God grows
deeper and your focus on knowing Him becomes sharper.
Your relationships with other believers also receive benefits as you enjoy community and fellowship together. As you
encounter God during these three weeks, my prayer for you
comes from the priestly blessing used for generations:

*Praying and fasting for 21 days is truly a spiritual adventure
unlike any other. Your commitment to God grows deeper and
your focus on knowing Him becomes sharper.*

"The LORD bless you
          and keep you;
the LORD make his face shine on you
          and be gracious to you;
the LORD turn his face toward you
          and give you peace."
     (Numbers 6:24–26 NIV)

seventeen

creating the prayer shield

—————

Pray often; for prayer is a shield to the soul . . .
a sacrifice to God, and a scourge for Satan.

—John Bunyan

In my twenties, I served as a youth pastor for a church in Colorado Springs, Colorado. There I met Wanda Elliott, a woman whose prayers had power like I had never seen. When I think of the prayers of the righteous being powerful and effective (James 5:16), I think of Wanda. In her sixties when we met, she had the sweetest disposition and helped me and everyone around her immediately feel comfortable and appreciated.

I got to know Wanda when I started playing golf with her

husband, Art. He was a war hero and had retired to Colorado Springs, where he had served early in his military career. Art was my golfing buddy, and Miss Wanda became my prayer intercessor. It wasn't like I approached her and had to ask. She simply had this amazing gift of intercession and loved supporting me and my ministry through her prayers.

Miss Wanda could pray for three hours as if there was nothing to it. It just came naturally for her. She said that was how she knew she had the grace-gift of intercession, because it was so easy for her. I regularly gave her requests that needed prayer coverage, and she instinctively prayed for things I didn't even tell her.

The impact of her prayer ministry made a huge impression on me, and since that time I've always built my ministry on prayer. When I began leading a youth service on Wednesday nights at our church during that time, I invited all the teens and anyone else to come to my home for a Tuesday night prayer service. At least fifty kids would show up, and they became prayer warriors as we fulfilled our shared objective: to cover our Wednesday service the following night in prayer.

As attendance on Wednesday nights grew, so did the number of teens at my house on Tuesday evenings. Within a few months, we may have had the largest youth ministry west of the Mississippi! Hundreds of teens and young adults got saved, and many are in full-time ministry today. During our Tuesday prayer services, I shared with them the same teaching and prayer models that I've been sharing with you in this book.

When we launched Church of the Highlands, prayer became

the foundation for everything we do. I remember when we first moved to Birmingham how I would drive around the city to pray for people in all the homes, neighborhoods, and businesses I passed. Our interstate system literally circles round Birmingham, and it would take about an hour for me to drive one lap around the city while praying. I'd crank up the worship music and intercede for the people in our area.

Our team also practiced a lot of prayer walking, which we continue to do today. We would meet in a neighborhood or particular part of the city and choose a few blocks to walk and pray over. Sometimes we would focus on residential areas, and other times we lifted up all the workers and businesses in a particular area. Other times we might focus on a school, rec center, or playground, praying for all the children and families who frequented those spots.

These are just a few of the examples of how we—myself, my family, our church—pray over every aspect of our lives, our relationships, our ministry, and our city.

Building a Prayer Ministry

Learning to pray first and expanding the role of prayer in your life means developing what I refer to as a "prayer shield." Numerous psalms and other references in Scripture describe God as a shield around His people, their defender and protector: "But you, LORD, are a shield around me, my glory, the One who lifts my head high" (Psalm 3:3 NIV). Creating a prayer shield draws on this metaphor to build a network of people in your life who pray for you on a regular basis as you pray for them.

The importance of intercessors, prayer services, and prayer small groups cannot be overstated. While they're essential for anyone in full-time ministry, I believe they're just as significant for every Christian. For many years, I've been teaching pastors and church planters the necessity of building a prayer shield. Now I hope the same steps can inform and equip you to create your own network of prayer supporters who are willing to join you in saturating your life with prayer.

God never intended for life and ministry to be based purely in our natural world. We need miracles, signs, and wonders to create touchpoints to the spiritual realm. We need a daily outpouring of the Holy Spirit to empower everything we do. Prayer is the bridge to living in the spiritual world and unleashing God's power in our lives.

> Prayer is the bridge to living in the spiritual world and unleashing God's power in our lives.

Enlist Personal Intercessors

The term "prayer shield" isn't simply something I pulled from Scripture—the phrase was popularized by a series of books written by C. Peter Wagner in the late 1980s and early '90s. In fact, one of these books was entitled *Prayer Shield: How to Intercede for Pastors, Christian Leaders and Others on the Spiritual Frontlines.*

In this volume and others, Wagner shaped an entire generation, including myself, on the topic of prayer and all of its elements. He not only emphasized various ways to pray, including prayer walking and prayer mapping, but stressed the necessity of having prayer intercessors.

Wagner instructed believers to build a network of prayer intercessors supported by intercessors at three levels, or what he called I-1, I-2, and I-3. Based on his descriptions, I-3 prayer intercessors are people who love to pray but tend to be more casual, sporadic pray-ers. In my case, these include the hundreds of people who come to our Saturday morning prayer services at Church of the Highlands. They join in as their schedules allow and lift up our Sunday morning services, the visitors who might attend, and the lost in our community.

According to Wagner, an I-2 intercessor is a person who takes their intercessory role much more seriously. They love to pray regularly, usually daily, and often take long blocks of time to pray for specific needs in their own lives and the lives of others. These I-2 intercessors know many details of your life and lift them up but don't usually know the most personal and pressing needs you face.

Presently, I have more than 120 intercessors who reflect Wagner's I-2 designation. Each month I send them a newsletter sharing recent praise items along with specific requests for prayer that I ask them to focus on. Throughout an entire month in advance, they bathe in prayer all the big events, special services, and unique outreaches our church has coming up. These intercessors are essential to everything we do, and our church would not have the impact God has blessed us to have without this dedicated team of committed I-2 intercessors.

Finally, an I-1 intercessor is someone who receives a special calling from God to pray specifically for you. They not only know of the big events and ongoing needs in your life, but they also keep in close contact with you regularly and get updated on details of your life and ministry. These people are either individuals who come to you with a burden from God's Spirit for praying for you at this level, or they're someone you know well and have hand-picked as a prayer confidant. My dear Wanda Elliott, who's now in heaven, was this kind of prayer intercessor for me. I currently have five such people who pray for me at an I-1 level.

In our church we also enlist specific I-1 type prayer intercessors to cover different members of our staff and various ministries within our Highlands family. Every pastor on our team has at least three key intercessors, and every ongoing ministry, such as our student ministry, has assigned intercessors who cover all of it in prayer. As you can see, we take prayer as seriously as possible and consider it essential to anything and everything we do.

Build a Solid Prayer Ministry

In addition to enlisting these various kinds of prayer intercessors, it's important to be deliberate about bringing people together to pray regularly. Praying corporately unites people in their faith and brings them together before the throne of grace. The New

Testament church was started in a corporate prayer meeting and was sustained through corporate prayers meetings. Jesus told us:

> "Truly I tell you, whatever you bind on earth will be bound in heaven, and whatever you loose on earth will be loosed in heaven.
>
> "Again, truly I tell you that if two of you on earth agree about anything they ask for, it will be done for them by my Father in heaven. For where two or three gather in my name, there am I with them." (Matthew 18:18–20 NIV)

Large gatherings for prayer and praying in small groups are equally important in constructing and expanding your dedication to prayer. I call our congregation at Highlands to pray together corporately twice a year—in January and in August. I encourage people to fast during our 21 Days of Prayer at the beginning of each new year. In August, typically the start of a new season for school and small groups, we pray together and I encourage people to feast on and celebrate God's goodness.

Every morning at 6 a.m. during our 21 Days of Prayer, we conduct prayer meetings at our various church locations. We begin with a few minutes of praise and worship together before sharing a brief devotional. We then have fifteen minutes of corporate prayer led by a pastor, followed by thirty minutes designated for individual prayers. We make sure to end promptly on schedule so that everyone can get to work or school on time.

Throughout the year, not just during the 21 days, we conduct similar Saturday morning prayer services. We often have several thousand people attend these at various locations. They come together to lift up that weekend's services, upcoming events and outreaches, needs in our communities, and other current events and concerns. This group of people also prays over individual prayer request cards we receive from our congregation every week. We also encourage this group to pray for those they know who do not yet know God to encounter Him and invite Jesus into their lives.

We also have a prayer team that is available in every church service to pray for anyone who has a need. This team is a part of our "Dream Team," the volunteers who use their gifts to make every part of the church stronger and better. As people go through the process of discovering their God-given gifts and purpose, many of them recognize that they are called to pray, and this is how they serve on the team.

Our church also has specific small groups focused on prayer. They might study prayers in the Bible or focus on specific aspects of prayer. All our small groups, no matter what their topical focus might be, spend some time in prayer for one another.

Watchmen on the Wall

In addition to prayer intercessors and prayer groups, some people are called to be "watchmen on the wall." These people cry out day and night to God and remain in continual prayer throughout their days. They are like the watchmen described in Scripture: "I have posted watchmen on your walls, Jerusalem; they will never be silent day or night. You who call on the LORD, give yourselves no rest, and give him no rest till he establishes Jerusalem and makes her the praise of the earth" (Isaiah 62:6–7 NIV).

Prayer watchmen are often essential to ongoing projects and times of transition. There's the great story of Nehemiah and the people of Israel trying to rebuild their country after returning from exile in Babylon. They found their homeland in ruins and had to start over, rebuilding the wall around Jerusalem to restore its defenses and establish its boundaries.

We kept at it, repairing and rebuilding the wall. The whole wall was soon joined together and halfway to its intended height because the people had a heart for the work. When Sanballat, Tobiah, the Arabs, the Ammonites, and the Ashdodites heard that the repairs of the walls of Jerusalem were going so well— that the breaks in the wall were being fixed—they were absolutely furious. They put their heads together and decided to fight against Jerusalem and create as much trouble as they could. *We countered with prayer* to our God and set a *round-the-clock* guard against them.

But soon word was going around in Judah,

The builders are pooped,

the rubbish piles up;

We're in over our heads,

we can't build this wall.

And all this time our enemies were saying, "They won't know what hit them. Before they know it we'll be at their throats, killing them right and left. That will put a stop to the work!" The Jews who were their neighbors kept reporting, "They have us surrounded; they're going to attack!" If we heard it once, we heard it ten times.

So I stationed armed guards at the most vulnerable places of the wall and assigned people by families with their swords, lances, and bows. After looking things over I stood up and spoke to the nobles, officials, and everyone else: "Don't be afraid of them. Put your minds on the Master, great and awesome, and then fight for your brothers, your sons, your daughters, your wives, and your homes." Our enemies learned that we knew all about their plan and that God had frustrated it. And we went back to the wall and went to work. From then on *half* of my young men worked *while the other half stood guard* with lances, shields, bows, and mail armor. Military officers served as *backup* for everyone in Judah who was at work rebuilding the wall. (Nehemiah 4:6–16 THE MESSAGE, emphasis added)

Whether you're rebuilding your life, your family, your career, your ministry, or some other endeavor, asking others to join you in your reconstruction or new venture is essential. Half may be involved in doing hands-on work while half pray and stand guard as spiritual warriors. This is the ultimate kind of prayer shield, literally creating a barrier against the forces of darkness as you conduct the Lord's work.

Praying each day is essential. Praying and fasting for 21 days brings you even closer to God's power and presence. But God is also looking for what I like to call "Day 22" people—the ones who

God is also looking for
what I like to call "Day
22" people—the ones
who are still praying
with the same fervor and
dedication throughout
the year, covering the
rest of us as we get back
to the work of ministry
and serving where God
leads us to serve.

are still praying with the same fervor and dedication throughout the year, covering the rest of us as we get back to the work of ministry and serving where God leads us to serve.

You Know What to Do

As you consider what it means for you to pray first, remember that prayer is relational as well as spiritual. Praying together has power and unleashes God's Spirit to work in churches, organizations, businesses, neighborhoods, cities, states, and nations. As you enlist intercessors and consider interceding for others, remember to also come together with others to pray on a regular basis. Consider if you're called to be a watchman on the wall, praying and supporting others continually in advancing God's kingdom.

If you want to know God at a deeper level, if you want to follow Jesus for the rest of your life, if you want to make a difference for eternity, then you know what to do.

Pray without ceasing.

Pray with other people.

And always *pray first*!

Acknowledgments

To all my friends who offered support, encouragement, and assistance on this project, I am more grateful than you'll ever know. I'm especially indebted to:

My wife, Tammy: You have been so loving and supportive in everything I have ever done. You are a gift from God and I will love you always.

My assistant Katy Smith: I simply couldn't do what I do without your help. Thank you for your hard work and devotion. You are such a blessing to me.

My writing partner, Dudley Delffs: Thank you for being a part of my life and ministry. Once again you captured my passion for this project and helped me express it on the page.

My agent, Matt Yates: Thank you for the encouragement, insight, and wisdom you provided throughout this entire process. I'm so grateful for your friendship and support.

The team at Thomas Nelson: Your partnership continues
to bless me. I'm especially grateful for my editor, Janene
MacIvor, and her dedication to making this book the
best it can be. It's a joy to work with you.

The team at Highlands—Kellen Coldiron, Katie Vogel,
and Chris Hanna: Thank you for your invaluable
contributions and for making me better.

My pastor Larry Stockstill: Your love for God and passion
for prayer has inspired me for more than forty years.
Thank you for teaching me how to pray.

My Savior and Lord, Jesus my King: It is a privilege
to do what You've called me to do. Thank You for
choosing me.

Notes

1. Jennifer O'Herin, "Prayer Closet," *What Then Why Now* (blog), August 8, 2017, https://whatthenwhynow.org/prayer-closet/.
2. "The 10 Most Dangerous U.S. Cities: 5. Birmingham," *Forbes*, October 18, 2012, https://www.forbes.com/pictures /mlj45jggj/5-birmingham-ala/?sh=b1562dd590f0.
3. Suzanne Wu, "Fasting Triggers Stem Cell Regeneration of Damaged, Old Immune System," University of Southern California: *USC News*, June 5, 2014, https://news.usc.edu/63669 /fasting-triggers-stem-cell-regeneration-of-damaged-old -immune-system/.
4. Gustav Niebuhr, "President of Campus Crusade Gets $1 Million Religion Prize," *New York Times*, March 7, 1996, https://www .nytimes.com/1996/03/07/us/president-of-campus-crusade -gets-1-million-religion-prize.html.
5. Bill Bright, "Your Personal Guide to Fasting and Prayer," *Cru*, accessed June 9, 2022, https://www.cru.org/us/en/train-and -grow/spiritual-growth/fasting/personal-guide-to-fasting.html.

About the Author

Chris Hodges is the founding and senior pastor of Church of the Highlands. Under his leadership, Church of the Highlands has launched campuses all across the state of Alabama and has grown to more than 60,000 people attending weekly. He also cofounded the Association of Related Churches, launched a coaching network called GROW, and serves as chancellor of Highlands College, a two-year ministry training college. Chris and his wife, Tammy, have five children and eight grandchildren and live in Birmingham, Alabama.